T0193457

MASTER PILOT

The Johnny Hruban Story

JOHN RAYMOND HRUBAN CFII

Order this book online at www.trafford.com
or email orders@trafford.com

Most Trafford titles are also available at major online book retailers.

Print information available on the last page.

ISBN: 978-1-6987-1511-7 (sc)
ISBN: 978-1-6987-1510-0 (e)

Library of Congress Control Number: 2023914951

Trafford rev. 08/17/2023

www.trafford.com
North America & international
toll-free: 844-688-6899 (USA & Canada)
fax: 812 355 4082

This autobiography was written by John R. Hruban in 2006 and published posthumously in 2023. I volunteered to edit and publish the manuscript to celebrate the Dick and Rosalie Lippincott Aviation Section opening of the Merrick County Museum. Rex and Leanne Luebbe have generously funded the project. Dan and Brian Tyler have added personal written contributions.

Randy Lippincott

Contents

Of Note, The Cover

The blue color of this book represents our ethereal and precious sky. This work's thin covering, like the earth's atmosphere, will last a lifetime if treated with respect. We are surrounded by a beautiful and mysterious gaseous medium that has given us life and facilitated the gossamer freedom of flight. The wild-blue yonder has been the sphere that has guided travelers through many wonderful sights, experiences, and even through time. Like the flight log, the book covering is functional, durable, and designed for frequent use. The lack of pattern symbolizes the fair weather blue sky and the hope of smooth travel and a safe journey. The acid-free paper should not yellow during your ownership. The pages are stark white like the snow-covered prairie and the expansive midwest that nurtured and challenged the young John Hruban. With little effort, you will find that these stories hold many of his secrets. I hope that sharing them with you will make them more valuable and help you understand the path from Johnny Hruban's perspective.

In addition, print size was selected to be more kind to the Boomer crowd. We often need to avoid print that we must strain to read. Youths should learn this functional lesson.

Dedication

Family -

This autobiography is dedicated to my children Judy Kracl and her two sons Marek and Alex in Lincoln, Nebraska; Tony, Julie, and their three children, Nicole, Ben, and Sarah, who live in Omaha, Nebraska; and Gina, who lives in Kansas City. I hope everyone will take the time to read it and keep it for future generations.

Each one of you has given me much joy and gratification. I am truly blessed.

—John Raymond Hruban, Master Pilot
December 9, 1930 - April 11, 2019

Prologue

Master Pilot by John R. Hruban is the third book of a Central Nebraska aviation anthology. The first, released in 1996, is called *Sharpie The Life Story of Evelyn Sharp - Nebraska's Aviatrix,* written by Diane Ruth Amour Bartels. Raised in Ord, Nebraska, Evelyn took her first flight lesson when she was fifteen and soloed one year later. Cut from the same fabric as Johnny Hruban. Sharp earned her private license at seventeen and a commercial-transport license at eighteen. By age twenty, she was one of only ten women flight instructors in the United States. Evelyn taught aviation to over 350 men in the Government's pre-WW II Civilian Pilot Training Program in South Dakota and California. When the War Department organized the Women's Auxiliary Ferrying Squadron in 1942, Sharpie qualified as its seventeenth member. She was destined to fly military fighter planes in a non-combat role.

Fifty Years Fly By author Randy Lippincott, 2017, is the second book in the local trilogy that helps establish the Merrick County flying story—his lifetime of not-so-fair weather, accident-free, incident-free aviation all started with John Hruban's calculated hours of instructing the basics. It is all about Randy's unique half-century of aviation and how he started flying with his family on the farm when he was five. The book transports you to all the places it took him, the close calls, and the thrilling high points, including 5,000 incredible hours flying as a Bush Pilot in Alaska. It was 14-hour-days at 45° below zero, less than four years to accomplish, and a lifetime to experience. His outstanding literary effort culminates with 8,000 total flight hours and the prestigious Wright Brothers Master Pilot Award presented in May 2016. On that day, as a Chief Warrant Officer Army Special Forces veteran, and following the Nebraska Navy Admiralship presentation, in one fell swoop, Randy became Chief, Master, and Commander. No small feat for a farm boy from Nebraska.

Master Pilot by John R. Hruban rounds out the museum's trifecta. His autobiography encapsulates Johnny's life story. It may start with motorcycle and stock car racing but rapidly switches to flying and the godfather of Merrick County aviation, Amos Sigfrid Bankson. It all started with the eccentric Amos. Johnny unabashedly describes his quest for the next aviation license upgrade and the flood of students he competently mentored. All the while, he was raising a family and looking for the upcoming best-flying gig. Intertwined with working as a florist and an authoritative five-year Federal job, Hruban earned the NTSB Outstanding Performance Award in 1989. During a phone call in 2012, while discussing this book, I told Johnny about the MPA and nominated him without hesitation. Ultimately, he was most proud of the prestigious and well-earned Wright Brothers Master Pilot Award presented to him in September 2013.

Upcoming Merrick County books. I am laying down the challenge of at least two additional adventure-filled

Merrick County aviation books between Dan Tyler, Brian Tyler, and Loren Lippincott. They all have stories and can articulate them. Dan, of course, has real war stories from Vietnam AND a lifetime of adventure flying helicopters in Australia - "Indiana Jones style." Brian has lived the dream, spanned the globe, and can share many real-world experiences to entice today's youth to take up commercial flight. As an Air Force F-16 fighter pilot in Europe, Loren was Top Gun. Everyone has seen the movies. It's foolish for me to try and add to that.

—Randall L. Lippincott, Master Pilot

Foreword

A little over a decade ago, I traveled from my home in Australia back to the USA for the Nebraska deer season and my annual recurrent training in a full-flight helicopter simulator located at DFW Airport in North Texas.

I remained in Texas for another few weeks to help with maintenance test flying on a new helicopter my Australian employer had bought. It was undergoing major service and being fitted out for rescue and medical work at a facility north of DFW.

There weren't many hours involved in that test flying, so I decided to take the opportunity while there to renew my Federal Aviation Administration (FAA) Certified Flight Instructor (CFI) rating that had lapsed after I moved to Australia almost forty years earlier. I also added an instrument instructor (CFI-I) to my list of American pilot ratings.

In studying for the instructor rating renewal exam at a local helicopter flying school, I refreshed myself on an important principle of instruction learned years earlier: The "Primacy Principle," – also known as the "Doctrine of Primacy."

I had mainly worked as an operational pilot for most of my flying career in Australia and hadn't given much thought to methods of instruction. However, I had been appointed to a Training and Checking position a year earlier and needed to get my head back into an instructional mindset.

The primacy behavioral principle can be expressed as: "first in – first out." The first thing we are taught about something will be what we remember the longest – and recall the quickest. The first learned reaction to a set of circumstances will be what we do if those circumstances occur in an emergency, even without conscious thought.

This principle is important in pilot training because – when a real in-flight emergency occurs – a pilot may be so overwhelmed with the drama of the situation as to have no cognitive space left to analyze the problem and formulate a solution. We simply react the way we have been taught at the outset. If what we were taught in the beginning is inappropriate – we'll probably do it anyway in the moment's agony – maybe with disastrous results.

Fast forward a couple of years to 2016, and I reached the 50th anniversary of my first solo flight under the supervision of John Hruban – my first flying instructor at Central City Municipal Airport in Nebraska. In that 50 years, I had flown over 11,500 hours – mainly on helicopters and typically in high-risk operations such as combat, search and rescue, firefighting, and law enforcement – all without an accident or a violation. I'd experienced a few in-flight emergencies in that time – but all had culminated in a safe landing.

That record qualified me for the FAA Wright Brothers Master Pilot Award. I was nominated by my brother Brian, who had started his flying lessons with Johnny Hruban, and by Randy Lippincott, who had learned to fly from Johnny only two months before I started my lessons at the Central City grass airfield.

My employer heard about the FAA award and sent out a press release. An Australian journalist came around to interview me. She asked what did I owe my good fortune of having flown half a century and almost 12,000 hours without an accident or a violation?

I thought about my father's guidance and assistance – as a WW-II bomber pilot who took up flying for pleasure almost twenty years after the war and took me on my first flight. I also considered my primary flight instructor from the Army Helicopter Training School at Fort Wolters, Texas. But – mindful of the Primacy Principle – I felt that I owed a particular debt of gratitude to Johnny Hruban – my first instructor who had trained and coached me through to my Airplane Private Pilot Certificate even before I graduated from High School and well before I joined the Army to fly helicopters in Vietnam.

When Randy Lippincott first told me about the Wright Brothers Master Pilot Award, he mentioned that he had searched the records. As far as he knew, John Hruban was the first Merrick County, Nebraska pilot to receive that award. Randy became the second recipient in early 2016, and a few months later, I became the third recipient from Merrick County (as far as we can determine). In 2020, my younger brother, Brian, having soloed on his 16th birthday and later flown 40 years for United Airlines (including about a decade and a half flying wide-bodied jets on international routes), became the fourth Merrick County native to receive the Master Pilot Award in 2020.

That the last three local recipients of the Master Pilot Award all learned to fly from the first recipient of that award in Merrick County – must reflect great credit on Johnny's skill as a teacher and his personal dedication to air safety.

Johnny's story – told in his own words – provides the reader with a unique opportunity to understand and absorb an exceptional aviator's genuine love of flying, perfectly balanced with his profound respect and appreciation of the risks in aviation. That Johnny so skilfully navigated a lifetime of flying adventures while sending so many aspiring aviators off on the right course – is another great tribute to a remarkable man to whom I am greatly indebted.

—Daniel E. Tyler, Master Pilot

About the Author

I am Judy, John's oldest child. I lived in Central City until after the 7th grade, so I remember quite a bit about the airport. We always loved any opportunity to go out there with Dad. It was fun to see whatever plane was there or the new solo shirt tails pinned to the wall. I did not inherit his love of flying. I get airsick. Despite that, we did take some long flying trips as a family. We flew to Ft. Lauderdale, Florida, and Dallas, Texas, and had many shorter trips.

Dad had a lot of jobs in aviation throughout his life. I know he enjoyed them all, but instructing was probably his favorite. John loved to share his passion with others and see them succeed, whether they got their private license or became commercial pilots. I know he supported the students who struggled with specific parts and could not have been more proud when they conquered them. He was always excited to hear from former students; some became lifelong friends.

I will never forget his love of animals, gardening, the perfect martini, and the silly sayings that made me shake my head then and make me smile now.

—Judy Hruban Kracl

In The Beginning

It was a bit like professional wrestling, primarily just for the show. The crowd always needed someone to boo. Anyway, I took a hiatus from racing for a while. Around 1960 a local friend built a racing stock car and wanted me to drive it. I accepted the challenge and began racing once again. It was a perfect car. We were very successful, and I won several Main Events and Trophy dashes. I changed my racing attitude but still carried a sign on the vehicle, "Clean Cut Driving by Dirty John." I enjoyed driving, and winning wasn't hard to accept either. My sponsor and builder of the car were satisfied after winning so many races that he sold it.

I continued to drive for the new owners until I was in a horrible accident during a race that resulted in my hospitalization for one week in Columbus. Luckily no broken bones but a badly sprained back and bruises. The total cost was $300, covered by insurance. About two or three weeks later, I competed one more time, wearing a back brace, and won. The last time I raced, I felt I had proved a point. I finally retired. I had been racing motorcycles and cars for nearly 15 years. The responsibilities of a family changed everything. And aviation was becoming a more significant part of my life.

My Early Aviation Years

Like most boys, I was fascinated by airplanes. During World War II, I remember scores of bombers that would fly over Schuyler at a low level. The sounds and sights were awesome. Then came the ride in the little yellow Piper Cub airplane with Georgia. I had already begun building model airplanes and collecting toy airplanes. We played with them for hours. Later, while in the Air Force, I rode in commercial airliners and once in a B-25, a twin-engine bomber (the famous General Jimmy Doolittle flew off an aircraft carrier in the WWII Raid on Tokyo). Additionally, we used to go to small airports around Chandler, Arizona, look around, sit in airplanes, and dream. You could buy an actual flying aircraft for as little as $350. One man in a little Interstate Airplane said he would sell it to us for $600 and throw in the flying lessons. I wonder if he was an instructor. Later, I was hooked when we chartered a small plane to transport my father to Mayo Clinic. I started my flying lessons in Central City in April 1959.

Flying, At Last

There was a flight instructor living in Central City named **Amos Sigfrid Bankson**. He was an electrician by trade and an older bachelor. Amos owned a J-3 Piper Cub N42829. Based in an open hangar on a farm along Route 66, on the south side of the road west of Hordville, a nearby small town. He had several students and agreed to teach me. A bit of a strange man, he had been an instructor during the war teaching Naval students but had served as an infantry soldier in WWI. He would not make appointments, so I had to drive out to the farm after work, and if the weather was good, with no wind, and Amos felt so inclined, he would show up. What could go wrong?

The first student to appear would observe the preflight inspection of the airplane. Amos would fill the tank with gas, which was good for about three hours of flight. Next, he would hand prop to start the engine. There was no electric starter. Then the lessons began-only a half-hour per student. He never shut off the engine between students. As I mentioned, he was a little set in his ways.

Anyway, I eventually soloed in about six hours. If this sounds early, it was, but not necessarily because of my skill. We had no radios and no ground school instruction.

There was never any traffic. We never flew in any wind. We never performed a pre-flight inspection. We flew the pattern repeatedly until he felt we could take off and land safely. The airfield we flew from was 1,800 feet long, one-quarter mile, and no more than an alfalfa field. Wires were on one end, and the hangar and trees on the other-not a considerable margin for error for a student.

The Cub was the ultimate in simplicity. However, during my second lesson, we practiced power-off glides, and the engine quit. I remember thinking we would simply restart it. Then I realized that you had to prop it by hand. Amos said to open the doors, so I knew this was serious. If the plane flipped, we would be able to get out immediately. The result was a forced landing in a fallow cornfield. We busted through an old barbed wire fence but, incredibly, didn't nose over. He was in command, flying proficient "stick and rudder." After coming to a stop, he looked the plane over, hand-propped it, told me to wait there, and flew off, bouncing down the cornrows. It could take off in a very short distance with a single person on board.

He flew back to the airfield and told someone to drive over and pick me up. It was indeed a strange occurrence. Afterward, Amos asked me if the forced landing deterred me from continuing my lessons. Having survived far worse situations while racing, I, of course, said, "No." **Amos never kept any logbooks on us nor mentioned we were to get a flight physical before solo.** I purchased a pilot logbook at the Grand Island airport and kept a log of all my flights and what we did during the lessons. Amos would later have a lot of explaining to the Federal Aviation Administration. Amos was not following the government's aviation regulations.

It was during this time that my father's health was failing. I never told him about my learning to fly as I felt he had enough on his mind. I had already caused him to have plenty of gray hair with my other activities, racing. Perhaps he knew, but now I'll never know for sure. My father also was inclined toward aviation. During World War I, he was discharged from military service before he could enter the Army Air Corps to fly.

After accumulating several hours of solo time and knowing what problems could arise with Amos's negligence, I started looking for an airplane to buy. I purchased a '48' Luscombe in Iowa. It was a little all-metal airplane, instead of fabric like the Cub, and had 65 horsepower but was a hot rod compared to the Cub. It would cruise almost 100 miles per hour, compared to the Cub's 65 mph. Amos didn't think much of my choice and said I would kill myself in it. He thought the Piper Cub was the ultimate flying machine.

The Luscombe was tied-down outdoors at the Grand Island airport, and I hired a new instructor to continue my training. Grand Island was an old airbase used for training by military bombers during WWII. It was a triangle of three long concrete runways, each over one mile long and like many others in the state. It differed considerably from the pasture where I gained my initial experience. About a year later, I sold the Luscombe and bought another that I found in York, Nebraska. It only had 350 hours total time and was just like new. All metal and nicely polished, it was a delightful airplane. And it had 85 horsepower, which made it a good cross-country airplane cruising at nearly 110 miles per hour. I earned my private pilot's license in it. Now, finally, I could take passengers. JoAnn and I flew to Big Springs, Texas, to visit my sister Gustie for a few days. I also flew Mom to Moberly, Missouri, once so she could visit a friend there.

I was happy being a private pilot for a few years until Central City, Nebraska, constructed a municipal airport. I decided to become a flight instructor and capitalize on the upcoming opportunity. Amos would never move to the new airport nor change his ways, which he didn't. I could make a profitable hobby by teaching others to fly, and I was correct. Working full-time running the florist business, I continued to fly. I began looking for flight schools to attend to complete my training. It was in early 1963.

Training For Additional Ratings

I earned money for additional training when I sold my airplane. At first, I took lessons whenever able in Grand Island, but it became apparent that this would take forever. Therefore, after investigating available flight schools, there were few in those days, so I enrolled at Ross Aviation, near Tulsa, Oklahoma. I would fly their Piper Colt and receive some dual in my first retractable geared airplane, a Piper Comanche. After a few weeks, I enrolled at American Flyers in Ardmore, Oklahoma. They had a superior curriculum. My initial aircraft was the Cessna 140A. Ground school was part of the curriculum, and I could pass the commercial and flight instructor written exams. I wanted to finish my flight time, get my ratings, and return home. The commercial and flight instructor's ratings were earned in Nebraska.

Now I could teach and charge for my lessons. I bought another airplane, a Piper Cub, but soon realized I could not take a student to obtain his private pilot's certificate, as it had no radios nor proper instruments required by the FAA. I did teach several people to fly in it, as far as I could take them. I sold it for $1,100. I taught the buyer to fly all the way up to solo. It only took him four hours of dual flight instruction. He was a very apt student, or I was an excellent instructor. Probably, a little of each. Next, I bought a 1948 Cessna 120 with the necessary radios and instruments to complete private training.

I could not base my airplane at the new Central City airport at that time, as no hangars were available. Initially, they built only six, which were all rented. Later, they would build additional hangars. I was parked at a small private grass airstrip near Marquette, Nebraska. It was located eight miles south of Central City. The owner had an airplane, and there was fuel available. I was accumulating students by then and was considering an aviation career. I also would fly for Norm Anderson, a Piper dealer in Grand Island. I would fly charters and give flight instructions. My pay was a total of three dollars an hour for flight time only.

However, I did have the opportunity to fly complex airplanes such as the Comanche 250 and a Cessna 182. I flew for Norman as needed, but sometimes it was almost full-time. Watching the classified ads in the <u>Trade a Plane</u> publication, I read an ad that called for a flight instructor and charter pilot in Norfolk, Nebraska. I applied and was hired. It was my first real pilot job. I began working, living with the airport mechanic, then after a few weeks, I rented a home and moved my family there. I was no longer in the florist business, with flying, as only a hobby. I also needed to resign from the Central City volunteer fire department since I would no longer be living there. I was still close enough to Central City, so I could help my mother out as needed. She continued to operate the florist business.

My Early Experiences In Norfolk

The names of my new boss and his wife were John and Helen Youngheim. The Fixed Base Operators (FBO) in Norfolk, Nebraska, also had a Cessna dealership, three four-place 172s, and one Cessna 150 trainer. It was a full-service FBO with gas and a full-time aircraft mechanic, Chuck Nerem. I stayed with him initially before moving my family there. John was an FAA-designated flight examiner and could give checkrides. He had vast experience as a pilot and was also a crop sprayer. John walked with a bad limp as his foot was partially amputated while crop dusting. The fan that drives the pump for the chemicals, located outside the cabin under the rudder pedals, failed while he was flying. A blade came up through the floor and almost amputated his foot. It was difficult for him to fly for any duration, so this was probably the reason for the hired help. I learned a tremendous amount from my association with him. His wife, Helen, was the office manager. Their workroom was in the terminal building along with the U.S. Weather Bureau and the North Central Airlines ticket agent. I earned an hourly wage, flying or not.

My initial work mainly was instructing in the Cessna 150. Then I was responsible for more and more charter flights. At first, shorter ones like Omaha, Lincoln, and

Grand Island, then more distant trips. I flew patients to Mayo Clinic in Rochester, Minnesota, and passenger flights to Fort Collins, Colorado, Wichita, Kansas, Grand Forks, North Dakota; and many other places. I flew numerous charter flights to Nebraska football games in Lincoln. One of my passengers was Norbert (Nobby) Tieman, who became Governor of Nebraska. I flew with morticians to pick up bodies. I had many exciting and challenging flights during this time. Night flying, sometimes during long cross-country flights, and flying in marginal visual conditions. It was risky but, at the same time, built confidence.

I remember one flight, especially as I had to fly a passenger to Grand Island and back in his airplane. It was in a freezing drizzle, with a 600-foot ceiling and one-and-a-half miles of visibility. About an inch of ice was on the wings when I got back—a deadly situation, not fun or safe. Luck was on my shoulder that day. Then, it was flying when I had equipment failures and many flights without an instrument rating during instrument conditions. Again, never a good idea. I made unscheduled landings on many rural airports and private landing strips. As required, I flew other makes and models, such as the slippery and capable 6-place Cessna 210 retractable. I also helped the mechanic when necessary. I had about 500 hours of flight time when I started this job. (Five-hundred flight hours is the most dangerous time in a flying career. You are competent enough to meet the challenge but lack experience on where to draw the line). When I left, I accumulated almost 900 flight hours. In about six months, I had flown over 400 hours. Many of them during the winter months, in hazardous conditions. I made many lifelong friends there and was lucky to have John Youngheim as a mentor.

JoAnn and my three children lived in our rented home. Judy was the only one old enough to attend school. Gina was relatively small, and Tony was too young to start school. We owned one car and a small motorcycle. Depending on the weather, I cycled to work as often as possible. Norfolk was about 80 miles from Central City, so we could visit there frequently.

The Wright Brothers
"Master Pilot" Award

presented to

John Raymond Hruban

in appreciation for your dedicated service, technical expertise, professionalism, and many outstanding contributions that further the cause of aviation safety.

September 2013

John's Master Pilot Award
Randy Lippincott photographer

In March 1965, I resigned and returned to Central City. Spring florist business was around the corner, and my mother would need our help. I returned to Central City to assist at the flower shop and continued to schedule flight instructions. More hangers had been built at the airport, so one was available for me. I had sold my Cessna 120 when I went to Norfork, so I started looking for another airplane.

We lived in Central City, in the original large house next to the old greenhouse, from March 1965 until moving to Schuyler in 1970. During this time, I taught Dick and Rosalie Lippincott all the way to their private license. And what was to become, years later, the following "Master Pilots," Randy Lippincott, Dan, and brother Brian Tyler, all mirrored my award from 2013. Randy's brother Loren Lippincott instructed in the Air Force and flew the F-16 for a total of 1,000 hours over ten years. He became a Captain at Delta Airlines in the Boeing 757-767 for a total of 30 years. Senator Loren D. Lippincott would have been the fifth Merrick County Master Pilot. In a way, they were all my students. I had done something right for the three farm boys to attain this crowning achievement.

Randy's Master Pilot Award
Randy Lippincott photographer

Flying In Central City

Also, in March 1965, I purchased a Cessna 140 but continued to operate out of the airport in Marquette from March 1965 until finally, I could hangar in Central City in June of 1967. I taught in Marquette, Central City, and Grand Island during this period. Most of the teaching around Central City and Grand Island was done other than on my airplane. I flew many makes and models of airplanes, including Taylorcraft, Piper, Cessna, Mooneys, Ercoupes, Aeroncas, and Beechcraft. They came in all shapes, sizes, and conditions. In December 1965, I flew a charter in a Cessna 182 for Robert Taylor, the movie star. I remember he sat in front beside me and told me he was also a pilot. His proximity made me quite nervous. During this period, my rates went from three to five dollars per flight hour of instruction.

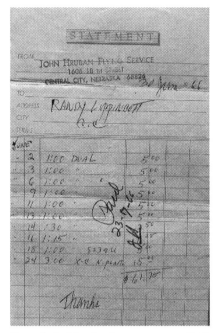

Randy's Flight Instruction Bill
Randy Lippincott photographer

In April 1965, I flew Tom McHargue, to Dallas, Texas, so that he could apply for a job as a mechanic for Braniff Airlines. Tom was hired, moved his family to Texas, and became an aircraft mechanic for Braniff. In July 1966, during a charter in the Cessna 140, I had an engine failure near Ida Grove, Iowa. I made a successful forced landing at the airport in Ida Grove. Fortunately, a commercial pilot was there with his airplane, and he flew me back to Central City. The next day I drove back 300 miles, removed the engine, and took it to Grand Island. It turned out the engine had a broken crankshaft, likely from an old unreported prop strike. I would be out of business while the power plant was rebuilt. However, this turn of events prompted me to buy a 1966 Piper Cherokee that Norman Anderson used as a trainer. Now I had a new, modern tricycle gear airplane that would carry four people, a great heater, and modern radios. My students were delighted, increased cost or not, and my business surged.

Later, one of Merrick County's Master Pilots, Randy Lippincott, recalled his solo flight under Johnny Hruban's instruction. As a 16-year-old, I learned by example from my parents. I flew from the same turf airfield where my mother and father had acquired their skills from Johnny. In nine hours, I practiced and soloed in a tail-dragger; it was the docile Cessna 140, N2479V. The all-silver bird had two large oval green-tinted skylights in the ceiling that were unusual and could be distracting for a youngster. While researching this story, I learned that the 1948 Cessna Model 140 I soloed in was still flying in the Dallas, Texas, area. That was very reassuring news to me. I was anxious to solo and trusted Johnny enough to know he would teach me everything I needed to succeed. I learned about climbs, banks, descents, power management, and stalls. He taught me that the control wheel adjusted for airspeed, and the throttle was used to climb and descend.

I understood the safety and function of the airport traffic pattern and how to use it as a cue for power and flap settings in preparation to land. During repeated takeoffs and landings, I became familiar with how the runway should look during my approach to landing. The final critical piece of the puzzle was the landing flare. If you didn't get that right, then everything else was useless. Rotate too late, and you bounce off the runway and violently back into the air. Pitch up too early, and you stall above the ground, crash into it and bend the landing gear, or worse yet, flip over out of control. With any crash, there is a risk of fire. I had excellent motor skills for an adolescent and a daring attitude—no fear, I had already had my routine share of lacerations, concussions, and broken bones. The mechanical apparatus was my friend, and I was in control. With a bit of exposure and practice, I easily commanded the routine operation of the air machine. Now with a bit of rehearsal, I could land with predictable success. Johnny knew the time was right, and I had "mastered" the basics.

Regardless, it was a surprise when he told me to come to a complete stop and let him out in the middle of the runway. It was June 16, 1966. At first, I wondered why he wanted to get out of the plane, and then I realized he wanted me to solo. It's like a threshold I've been working toward but never imagined how it would look when I arrived. It was only momentarily awkward for me. Okay, I was a bit surprised, but I had been doing it all along. It was just that Johnny had always been with me, acting as my safety net. Now I had to do it all, preflight the airplane, run the checklist, make my announcements on the radio, AND look and listen for other traffic, taxi and take off—no problem. Oh yeah! And then land without bending the airplane.

Soloing is when the student pilot does three circuits in the traffic pattern accompanied by three takeoffs and landings as the plane's sole occupant. I remember my mother excitedly telling her lady friends that she soloed in the family airplane, and they asked, "Rosalie, where did you go?" This question exposes the genuine gap in perception and knowledge between the aviator and the naïve masses. Soloing is the first time you perform a series of takeoffs and landings all by yourself; you don't leave the pattern at the airport or GO anywhere. It is an operational litmus test in your student training and the palpable beginning of the actual learning process.

Ready for my first solo flight at the south end of the runway, I did my run-up to include the mag-check and a 360° turn to carefully look for other airplanes that might be in the traffic pattern and not have a radio. When I saw it was clear, I lined up at the end and released the brakes as I smoothly applied the power. Thinking back on it today, I was a 16-year-old kid ready to fly an airplane, off a grass strip, for the first time by myself. I had no video game training for this; it was all real-world activity with undeniable consequences. As I started rolling down the forgiving turf runway, I noted that my airspeed was "alive." Next, I applied slight forward pressure on the yoke and gently raised the tail off the ground with little effort. With only modest back pressure on the control wheel, I sprang off the tiny airstrip at the prescribed airspeed. Wow, the airplane was highly responsive without Johnny as my passenger. It made a striking difference in the aircraft's performance as I adjusted the trim tab for the climb-out.

I was at pattern altitude in a minute, turning onto my crosswind leg. I brought the power back and continued the downwind leg, now well-established in the traffic pattern. I had just enough time to readjust my trim, glance at the windsock and note that it was still flaccid. Directly abeam my touch-down point, I again adjusted the power, applied full carburetor heat, and my first notch of flaps. The small Cessna started to slow and descend; I was at the prescribed 500-foot level above the ground when I turned on the base leg.

Okay, so far so good. I was doing it just like I had learned with Johnny at my side. It was already a natural routine for me. Unfortunately, I started my turn on the final leg late and had to correct back as I applied full flaps and adjusted my airspeed. My altitude looked good; the runway picture was nearly perfect—even if the power quit right then, I could still land on the field. As I approached the end of the runway, I pulled the power back and gracefully settled onto the "centerline" of the green runway. Whew, that was actually kind of fun! Now I had to do it two more times to make it count as a full solo. And just like that, with slight variations, it came to pass. Johnny was there to congratulate me and endorsed the back of my student license along with my logbook. I was officially cleared to fly solo in my father's Cessna 140. All I needed was the key to the hangar, the airplane key, and a key to the gas pump. It was protocol to fill the gas tank and record it in a log in preparation for the next person and any future flights.

Throughout that same period Dan Tyler, the third Merrick County Master Pilot and son of a WW-II Pacific B-24 Liberator pilot remembered his training with Johnny. "I went for my first lesson on July 12, 1966. We flew in his Cessna 140 N2313V. Johnny told me that after we finished, he had a charter flight to carry a passenger to Mason City, Iowa. A few days later, when I tried to book my second lesson, Hruban told me that while overhead at Storm Lake, Iowa, en route to Mason City, 13V lost power. He was able to land safely at the Ida Grove Airport. He said that even though the crankshaft had fractured cleanly, there was enough friction from part of the crankshaft within the crankcase that the propeller was still turning at reduced power. That helped him stretch the glide to a safe landing."

At the time of Tyler's second lesson on July 22nd, Johnny had a new Piper PA28-140 Cherokee N6446R painted red and white to replace the Cessna 140. On August 11th, with 6.5 hours of dual instruction, Johnny soloed Dan in 46R at Central City (07K).

It Was An Error In Communication

Bruce Bedient described the following as an "educational experience." It was a simple communication error. The day was clear, and the wind was calm on the Central City grass runway. Bruce met Johnny Hruban for a flight, one of several flight lessons. After about half an hour of touch-and-go's in the Piper TriPacer, Johnny instructed Bruce to let him out for his solo flight. In the excitement, Bruce heard three landings and "take off." It was all very innocent. Of course, most pilots know you don't go anywhere on your first solo flight. You must learn to walk before you run. But, in the thrill of the moment, Bruce misunderstood what Johnny's instructions meant.

To Johnny Hruban's surprise and bewilderment, the young instructor watched three perfect touch-and-go's, and then Bruce left the pattern! He headed southeast over Central City towards Polk. However, Johnny had yet to learn of his intentions. As Bruce reached Polk, he dutifully switched fuel tanks. But, at that moment, the engine began sputtering. Bruce felt slightly panicked as he was already low-level and urgently looked for a place to set the aircraft down. He saw concrete close by and made an uneventful emergency landing. Ultimately, Bruce caught a ride back to Central City, and when he arrived at the Hruban office, there was a note for him. Johnny had gone to Grand Island to the Flight Service Station to report the incident. He could not wait any longer, and "Where in the world did you go?"

Since Johnny didn't have a second aircraft for search and rescue when Bruce was overdue, he directly notified Flight Service of the situation, and the clock was running. By the end of the day, the ordeal was resolved. Johnny demanded to know why he'd left the pattern on his first supervised solo. Bruce replied that he thought instead of saying he should make three take off's and landings, what Bruce heard was, make three landings, and then he could 'take off' (as in departing the pattern).

Earlier that day, Jean Steckmyer got involved as an experienced WWII B-17 Flying Fortress bomber pilot and club member. He drove to Polk to recover the little airplane. After checking it over, he fired it up, gave it a thorough run-up, and taxied as far to one end of the area as possible to make a short field takeoff. The advanced technique is to taxi as fast as practical toward the endpoint and then accelerate out of the turn while heading into any available wind. You gained a significant advantage versus taking off from a complete standstill. Jean uneventfully flew the familiar aircraft back to Central City. Bruce was in a club that owned the Tri-Pacer. It included Jean Steckmyer (WW-II bomber pilot), Dr. John Cambell, Bruce's brother Warren, and Leslie McHargue. Later, Johnny did sign Bruce off for his solo flight with an Asterix.

Following that experience, Bruce enthusiastically kept flying. He got a job at the York, Nebraska airport doing miscellaneous work and building flight time. He successfully earned his private pilot's license but never continued in aviation. It was not quite as exciting as the "First Solo." Farming and raising two children didn't allow for that sort of discretionary spending.

My student base increased, at one time, to 45 active students. They came from nearby towns of Fullerton, Genoa, Polk, Clarks, Grand Island, Aurora, and more. I remember one day when I logged 11 hours and 45 minutes. My new little Piper Cherokee worked great for charter flights, and it flew a training flight as far as Phoenix, Arizona. During these years and up to 1970, I completed the training for over 60 students. Mainly for a private pilot license, others for additional ratings, such as commercial and flight instructor. Many more never completed their training, but most had at least soloed. I did a lot of check-out flights for pilots learning to fly a new or different model airplane.

During that time, Rosalie Lippincott and Retha Treptow were Johnny's students in Central City. The following are excerpts from Rosalie's story, Who Me, Fly... An Airplane?

The first entry in my Pilot Logbook was dated November 28, 1966; first flight, effects of controls, John Hruben CFI 1484580 one hour. I had another 45-minute lesson the following day. The plane was our own Cessna 172, N8239U. At ten hours, I could take the bird around alone. I wondered what John thought about my abilities and wished he'd let me solo.

On February 14, we did several crosswind landings, but I knew he would only expect me to solo with little to no wind. The next lesson was on February 24, and I had some hood time, flew to Grand Island, where I handled the radio contact with the tower, and landed unaided on an unfamiliar field. Back we flew to Central City and did several go-a-rounds. John said, "O.K., stop after this landing, I'm going to get out, and you do three touch and goes."

My heart pounded. **THIS WAS IT**, the day I had become impatient for yet feared. I grabbed his arm. "Oh, no, please don't leave me!" He told me he would ride around one more time and for me to pretend he was not there. "You've been doing this alone for some time now, and you'll do just fine," he assured me. The next landing was perfect, and I stopped the plane. "How can you tell I am ready to solo," I asked? Maybe first to stall a little longer, he said, "I have a rule I use to determine if my student is ready for the solo flight. I think, would I put my children in the back seat and let them ride. Today, I would let them ride with you." Bless you, Johnny. At that moment, you said the very thing I needed to hear. Immediately I knew I could perform the solo flight. The first takeoff went smoothly, and the landing was O.K., although the plane did handle a little differently without a passenger in the right seat. After the second takeoff, it hit me that I was alone, on my own, but I made those three landings; all good if I do say so myself.

I am unable to describe the solo flight; that singular, solitary performance intended for one, an experience you cannot share. A woman, alone on my own for the first time as the plane lifted off the ground. No parent for protection, no boss for directions, no husband to lean on, and no doctor whose orders you must obey. An adventure I will always remember, but one I could not share with anyone who has not had a similar experience. Congratulations and a warm handshake from the instructor who had watched. I questioned what he had been thinking? No wonder he needed Tums and Rolaids. I hurried to the Treptows' for a sharing time. A girl had to tell someone! The next day Retha made her solo flight, and I know she felt the same heady, wonderful way I did.

Johnny was part of a flying club in Central City with six members, each owning 1/6 of a new Cherokee 180. He could use the airplane for charter and taught the other five members to fly it. It was a very successful venture, giving him another airplane to fly and rent. "We charged ourselves nine dollars an hour to use it, including gas—a real money maker."

My instruction also took me to Albion, Nebraska, about 50 miles north of Central City, about once a week. A group of nine men in Albion formed a club, then purchased an Alon Aircoupe to learn in—a little two-place, low-wing airplane. None of them had any previous training. Nor had I ever flown one of those airplanes. Not to worry, I flew my Cherokee to Albion and gave lessons to all that showed up that day—sometimes two, usually more. I would charge them accordingly for my flight there and back. We flew off of the Albion municipal grass airfield.

The Aircoupe turned out to be a great little airplane, and even in my absence and with no supervision, they never had any problems or accidents. In fact, one of the students, who was nearly ready to solo, went out to the airport one day and soloed himself. Not legal, of course. I soloed him again during his next lesson when it was pretty windy. He was somewhat nervous because of the flight conditions, and I never let on that I knew what he had done. Over 20 years later, the same airplane was advertised in the Topeka, Kansas, newspaper, and I drove over to look at it. I knew it was the same airplane as I examined the logbooks for validity. It was never damaged after all those years and was in excellent shape.

Barnstorming was a staple in my repertoire. I gave rides for a penny-a-pound at many a County fair. JoAnn would weigh the passengers, and I would give them a quick 10-minute ride. I gave dozens of people their very first airplane ride. One day I flew seven hours without getting out of the pilot seat. It was quite a bit of fun, but I was tired when we flew home. I did make money by doing this, but we certainly couldn't waddle around. Later I gave aerobatic rides also. However, only some were interested in those, as it's a wild ride: loops, rolls, spins, and the like. I always had a sick sack handy for a green passenger.

I sold the Cherokee to Jerry Shull in March 1967. He was a very good friend of mine that lived in Palmer, Nebraska. I trained him through his flight instructor rating. Tragically he committed suicide years later. I bought a new 1967 Cherokee in Vero Beach, Florida. We flew down in the club 180 Cherokee to pick it up. There were three students with me. The trip paid for expenses, and I made a little profit. Of the three students that went, all but one made careers in aviation. The third almost did but instead went into private enterprise.

Crop Spraying

In May 1967, I was approached by Alf Glaser of Spalding, Nebraska, to see if I wanted to become a crop sprayer. I agreed, and shortly after, with some training, I was furnished with a crop duster and support equipment. I began my new additional, and dicey career in crop spraying. This move was quite profitable and certainly enhanced my income. The airplane was a Piper Super Cub PA–18, a hopped-up edition of a Piper Cub, with a 150 horsepower engine and a 90-gallon spray tank (roughly a 630-pound additional payload) attached to the belly. It flew well, but it is known as The Widowmaker in the industry. There was very little protection in the event of a crash. It was said that if you survived your first year in this airplane, you were a genuine crop duster. I survived, but later, I had some very close calls.

I did not begin flying to provide myself with thrills and daring. It was not a substitute for racing cars and motorcycles. The only sense of speed one gets is during the takeoff and landing. However, crop spraying is close to racing because you are only a couple of feet above the fields. You fly over wires, under wires, and sometimes through them, nearly missing trees and other objects. Plus, the airplane is grossly overweight when you start out, and this compounds the risk. During summertime operations, density altitude may also be a factor. In the advent of a crash, you risk getting a chemical bath, and depending on what you were using, can be more deadly than the crash itself. I carried a respirator and the injectable drug atropine. It is to be used in case of a crash while carrying deadly insecticides such as parathion, a toxic nerve gas.

Alf bought a new CalAir A-9 for me to use. It was a state-of-the-art spray plane. I was to fly commercially to Jackson Hole, Wyoming, then drive to Afton and pick up the new airplane, which I did. It cruised at 80 miles an hour and had a two-hour fuel range, no radios or flight instruments, just the necessities—a compass, airspeed indicator, altimeter, and fuel and oil pressure gauges. I had to be careful with my flight planning as the first part was deep into the Rocky Mountains. I stopped in North Platte, Nebraska, near twilight to get a bite to eat. By then, it was dark, and when I returned to the airplane to leave, I noticed it had no lights. Interior or exterior. It occurred then that these planes were not designed for night flights. No problem, I went back to the café and picked up several books of matches, and took off for home. It was a dark, hazy night with limited visibility and no horizon. I flew over Highway 30 using the sparse automobile lights for reference. Pretty low, probably 500 feet, and I made it home. I would strike a match from time to time, in the dark cabin, to check my instruments. I had no flashlight, which is something I should've carried.

In the off-season, after spraying ended in the early fall, Alf would have me take charter flights in his Cherokee. I would also teach, sometimes in his 180 Cessna, and assist around his two airports. I helped construct a large hanger during that time.

Rosalie Lippincott's story continues here.

The first week in November 1967, John told Retha and me that we were ready for our checkrides with the FAA designee. He made an appointment with Thomas Umberger to come to Central City for that purpose. The day came November 9, and surprisingly I felt prepared. John had worked hard to have us ready. Instructor abilities in question, he appeared nervous. I had the necessary items: medical certificate, student pilot certificate, radio operators permit, written test results, computer, plotter, maps, flight plan, and log with the necessary hours. John had signed the log book and recommended the private pilot checkride. The operator's manual, aircraft registration, airworthiness certificate, and performance charts were all stored in the plane.

After I had performed the walk-around, Mr. Umberger instructed me to depart on a 120-degree heading. We began a flight to Beatrice, Nebraska, at the appropriate altitude. Then because of an emergency that he made up, we turned to Hastings. On the way, he told me to contact the Grand Island Tower. We flew on instruments, slow-flight, did a power-off stall, a 720-degree turn, and then returned to our home base and a perfect landing. "Now all that's left to do is to fill out the papers," he told me, and I asked,

Earn Wings In Flight Check

Two Central City matrons, housewives by vocation, are now wearing wings, sprouted last Thursday at Central City Municipal airport. Mrs. Dick (Rosalie) Lippincott (left) and Mrs. Kenneth (Rhetha) Treptow successfully completed check rides with an FAA flight examiner from Lincoln to earn private licenses. They join a very select group of women pilots in Nebraska and become only the second to be licensed in Merrick county. Mrs. Kathryn White preceded them a number of years ago. With them is their instructor John Hruban who began their training in November of 1966. Both ladies made solo flights in the latter part of March of this year, completing their solo cross country work this summer and the other training necessary to qualify for a flight check ride.
—Republican-Nonpareil photo

Rosalie, Retha, and John

"With your signature?" He said, "Yes, with my signature." My heart sang! I was so very proud of myself. A couple of months into my fortieth year, I had a brand new private pilot's license. I believe all our children were also very proud of their mother and her accomplishment... right kids? There were more congratulations as we hugged each other and our excellent instructor. In the Central City weekly paper, the Republican-Nonpareil had a hallmark picture of us, John, Retha, and Rosalie.

You Crack Me Up

I continued to spray until August 1968. **It was then that I experienced my first crash.** I had just made my initial heavily loaded spraying pass on a cornfield and was making my turnaround when the engine failed. After pulling up to slow and minimize the turning radius, I was about 150 feet in the air. Immediately I shoved the nose down to maintain airspeed and control, steered the airplane away from the farm buildings, and pointed into the wind. Then I crash-landed in a mature cornfield. After everything had come to a standstill, I assessed the situation. The plane was upright, with no smell of gas, no fire, and I felt that my lightning reflexes had saved the day.

I suffered no injuries, and the plane was not severely damaged. In fact, I assisted in repairing it the next year and continued to fly the same sprayer. Although I finished the preseason in the Super Cub, I decided to retire from the spray business. I experienced another event in the Super Cub when I struck some powerlines. Fortunately, the wires broke, but in slow motion, like drawing a bowstring. The airplane almost stalled, which would have resulted in serious bodily injury or worse. There was nothing for me to do - I was only an observer. It was over in an instant! Spraying paid very well, but I had a wife and family to consider.

My accumulated flight time was over 3,500 hours by then. All the while, I continued to run my Central City business. I was getting somewhat overwhelmed and approaching mental collapse. One man could only do so much. I decided to form a corporation and take on some partners. They were John Hall and Jim Hemmer, from Genoa, Nebraska. Both had been my students and owned airplanes. John owned a Piper TriPacer, and Jim a Piper Cub. John also helped me while I was crop dusting. He lost his right forearm as a child and wore a prosthesis, but could practically do anything a man with two arms could do. He also had his instructor's license. Their airplanes would add to our fleet along with our new Mooney. We became a dealer for Mooney aircraft in 1968.

Central City Flying Service, Inc.

Now, we had five rental airplanes to teach in. By training so many pilots, I created a tremendous rental base. I also assisted pilots in purchasing their airplanes. I would earn commissions for those transactions. In addition, I would rent larger planes from Grand Island when I needed more room or, in some cases, a stretcher patient or a body for the mortuary. I was appointed Airport Manager in Central City and later elected to the Airport Authority, the local governing board. The FAA instigated a new ruling regarding charter flying. I needed to obtain an instrument flight rating for night VFR flight. I also wanted my multi-engine rating and some aerobatic instruction.

Training In Florida

In January 1969, I drove to Fort Lauderdale, Florida, with my family. We had permission to take our children out of school for the time we would be there. We stayed with JoAnn's aunt, who lived in Fort Lauderdale. She was an accredited school teacher, so she homeschooled our children, which was accepted back in Nebraska. I enrolled in flight school there and flew every opportunity that I could. Many times I flew twice a day. I had to fly the required number of instrument flight hours and pass the written exam. I earned my instrument rating in less than two weeks. I also drove to Lantana, Florida, once a week to receive aerobatics lessons. That is where I learned loops, Chandelles, Immelmans, vertical reverses, Cuban eights, slow rolls, snap rolls, and precision spins. We flew out over the ocean to practice, which was a little weird for me.

My family had a great winter vacation in Florida, and I accomplished my objectives. Returning home, we stopped at Sowell Aviation in Panama City, Florida, and I took multi-engine flying lessons. I earned my multi-engine rating in three days. Then we returned to Nebraska.

Early Job Search

Charter flights and instruction were my bread and butter. I was swamped but started looking for a job with more of a future. I flew to Hot Springs, Arkansas, and met Art Cohn, who had an operation in Clearwater, Florida. He was looking for an all-around employee. I returned home, and he contacted me in a couple of weeks and agreed to hire me. I was to do flight instruction and sales. He wanted me to fly down to Hot Springs, pick up an older Cessna 172, fly it to Savannah for possible sale, and bring it to Clearwater if not sold.

My trip to Hot Springs was by commercial airline. I picked up the Cessna and departed for Savannah, Georgia. I arrived in Albany, Georgia, to refuel and get something to eat. It was dark when I left, and I had to fly over desolate swampland to get to Savannah. The radio was very poor and didn't have the proper frequencies to contact the Savannah Control Tower. Eventually, I contacted them on an alternate frequency. Then I had to roll up a chart and hold it to my ear, against the ceiling radio speaker, to understand anything that was said. Fortunately, it was pretty late by then, and there was minimal traffic. I was cleared to land. I stayed overnight in Savannah and showed the airplane to prospective customers the following day. They decided they didn't want it, so I fueled it up and continued to Florida. I had to land at a nearby, uncontrolled airport near my destination and telephone the control tower so they would allow me to land. As I said, the radio was very poor. Eventually, I arrived at my new job location.

Immediately, I began working for Art, mostly with flight instruction. I wasn't prepared to rent a room, as I only brought a few clothes or necessities. I was going down to determine if I wanted to do this. It was a pretty small operation with limited Aircraft to use. Since I didn't rent a room, I lived in the business office and slept on a bench seat. I shaved and cleaned up in the restroom, which only had cold water. Pretty miserable conditions overall. I ate when and where I could.

Return To Nebraska

Alf Glaser called me in Flordia and asked if I would return to Nebraska and work for him again. He would pay me a salary plus what I would make spraying. He also wanted me to fly up to Albany, Georgia, to pick up a new crop sprayer he had purchased. I agreed to do that, so I left Florida and flew commercially to Albany, Georgia, where the Rockwell Airplane factory was located. I had dinner with the sales manager, and he asked me if I would be interested in being a representative? They needed someone in the middle eastern territory. The conversation sparked my early thinking about trying to work for a manufacturing company.

The following morning I started my flight home in an airplane similar to the one I had previously flown for Alf. This was a long, arduous flight coupled with all the problems I could encounter while airborne—still an 80-mile-an-hour airplane with a two-hour fuel range. Finding fuel stops would become a real challenge. No radios, so all stops were to be in small uncontrolled airports. I did fly over a lot of interstate highways in order to read the signs. The statement was a joke among pilots, but it wasn't a joke in this case. I really did read the signs. Most of my flying was at 500 feet altitude, so seeing them was no problem. The flight would last 14 hours, but I did stop overnight in Salina, Kansas. When I got home, I began my new job with Alf again.

My Last Years In Central City

My last two years in Central City were a mixed bag of flying. I worked and flew for Alf Glaser, flying in Spalding, Albion, Central City, and Grand Island. I continued to do some crop spraying, but I had yet to do much as I had done before. I did whatever I could to continue to make a comfortable living. I flew charters to Wisconsin, Illinois, Texas, Minnesota, Missouri, and wherever I was asked. I delivered and picked up crop sprayers from Georgia, Kansas, and Iowa. I gave aerobatic instructions and performed at airport dedications. Elf bought an aerobatic Citabria so I could teach in it. My training in Florida was paying off.

Also, I began searching for a more lucrative job during this time. I made applications at several flying operations from California to Delaware. I was hoping for a factory representative position with an aircraft manufacturer. I flew down to Kerrville, Texas, along with my family, for an interview with Mooney Aircraft Company. I felt I had pretty much reached a saturation point where I was suffering from "burnout." I had taught about everyone that was warm and breathing, so the saying goes. A couple of years later, I would accomplish my goal of becoming a factory representative.

Meanwhile, Central City acquired funds for hard surfacing the airport runway. It was the late summer of 1970, which resulted in the airport closing for most flight activities. I could still use the grass sides of the runway to take off and land, but there were no lights on the runway, and night flying was impossible. I was, basically, shut down. That summer, the Lincoln Manor Steakhouse and Lounge operators in Central City broke their lease. John Hall asked if I would like to operate it until the owners found a buyer. Since the airport was closed, I agreed. His mother, aunt, and other relatives all had experience in restaurant operations and agreed to help us. John and I were to manage the eatery and be the bartenders.

It was an exciting experience; we both learned much about the restaurant and bar business. JoAnn would help as a hostess on Saturday nights, especially during the holidays. Occasionally I would have to organize a band and play when whoever was hired failed to show. It was usually Larry on the piano, Elf on the accordion, a drummer, and myself on the saxophone. We usually had live music on Saturday nights. John and I hired a bartender later, but we still helped on busy nights and at parties.

All in all, it was a fun experience. It paid the bills and made a little money. But I knew this wasn't the life for me, and although we could have purchased the business, I elected not to be involved. The business eventually sold, and the new owners took over on January 2, 1971. We had our last night of running the business on New Year's Eve. All our friends were there; overall, it was an experience to remember.

The Move To Schuyler

In prior discussions with my uncle Jim Hruban about buying his florist business, I started driving to Schuyler, working all week there, and then coming home for the weekend. Later, we decided to move, sold our house, and moved to Schuyler.

We bought a newer ranch home in a nice neighborhood, and I continued to work for Jim as an employee. I was paid two dollars an hour. JoAnn helped from time to time also. My mother Albina, who now lived in Schuyler, was Jim's full-time employee. I still had an airplane based in Columbus and continued to do occasional instruction and charters. I was checked out in the fixed base operators' airplanes there and had access to them. I joined a flying club and had additional access to three other airplanes. I hadn't given up on aviation yet.

Problems At Home

Jim decided to take a trip to his homeland in Europe and would be gone for six to eight weeks. While he was gone, we took this as an opportunity to completely remodel the office, lower the ceiling, paint the exterior, and move the work area from the basement to the upstairs. All in all a general renovation, which it needed badly. It was mostly rundown, as Jim only believed in improving it a little. We were delighted with the results and, of course, the convenience that it created. We accomplished all of the labor and did not have to hire any of the work done. During this time, we had to conduct business as usual, doing all the greenhouse chores, changing soil, planting, and mending the glass roof. In fact, we also had a hail storm which did considerable damage. I did the repair and all of the glass glazings in the greenhouse. The total cost of the paint, labor, and all materials was a little over $400. A paltry sum, although later Jim complained and thought it outrageous.

I misjudged my uncle. Upon his return, he was infuriated with what we had done. I knew then he had no plans of selling his business, at least not in the near future, and my time there would certainly be limited and under a great strain. I decided to do something else.

Our life in Schuyler was pretty respectable. My social life was good. We had a lovely home and two cars and lived in a nice neighborhood. We had wonderful neighbors with whom we became good friends. The children all went to school there, which was within walking distance from our home. The municipal swimming pool, tennis courts, baseball diamonds, and golf course were included. The kids all did well in school. Tony was in the band and played sports. Judy was in the girl's cheer squad, Gina was busy doing things she liked to do, and she was also a good athlete. Gina and Tony both took piano lessons.

JoAnn eventually started part-time work at the hospital in the medical records department. Something she would make a career out of later. She also helped at the floral shop as needed. I had a couple of small dirt bikes, which Tony and I would ride in the country. It was the beginning of his riding motocross competition, which lasted quite a few years. I also bought Gina a little children's motorcycle so she could tag along. Tony and Gina loved to ride. We bought Judy a 1967 Mustang for her 16th birthday. Albina and Uncle Jim were married around 1972, furthering my belief that he wouldn't be ready to sell out soon.

Vaughn's Seed Company

After seeing an ad in the Florist Review magazine, I sent a résumé to Vaughn's Seed Company, of Downers Grove, Illinois, near Chicago. They were one of the nation's largest suppliers of florists in greenhouse stock. Vaughn's sold everything from seeds, bulbs, plants, foliage plants, fertilizers, greenhouse construction materials, and more. I was immediately notified by phone that they had an opening and asked that I fly out to Chicago for an interview. I presented for the interview and was promptly told that I could work for them as a regional salesman. My territory would be Kansas, Missouri, and Northern Oklahoma. I was given a draw against commission, car mileage, and expenses.

Straight away, I bought a new car, which I would put in excess of 50,000 miles a year on. After initial training, I had no problems performing my job. After all, I had spent much of my life in the florist and greenhouse business. I did, however, not care for the job as I was gone all week and had to drive a considerable amount. I drove as much as 600 miles daily, in addition to four sales calls. The pay was excellent, and I cultivated many friends with my customers and those I worked for. I traveled to Florida, Colorado, and Texas, plus many trips to Chicago. While in Florida, at a foliage show, I rented an airplane and flew two of my best customers from Overland Park, Kansas, to the Bahamas. But the idea of waking up Monday morning and knowing I had to drive back to Kansas to enter my territory didn't sit well with me.

After one year, the territory I was living in opened up, and they transferred my responsibilities to Nebraska, North, and South Dakota, and western Iowa. If anything, this would require me to drive more miles each year. I wasn't particularly happy about all this, even though I lived in my territory now. I did use the airplane several times to call on customers, but it wasn't a practical way to make contacts.

It was late 1972 when I responded to an ad that Grumman American Aircraft Company had put in the Omaha paper. They wanted a sales representative in my area. I sent a handwritten résumé and was immediately contacted to fly out to Cleveland, Ohio, for an interview. I could not have been happier. Here was my chance to do what I did best. I was hired and would have the 12 North-Central states as my responsibility.

My Job With Grumman American Aircraft Company

In January 1973, I went to Cleveland, Ohio, to begin my training as a regional sales manager for my assigned territory. I was given check flights in all the airplanes they built and sold. My familiarization included all the manufacturing techniques and characteristics of the airplanes. I met with all the company personnel that I would be working with. Of course, I was introduced to all the necessary paperwork that I would have to be familiar with. I was also interviewed by the CEO Russ Meyers, before being hired. Later he would become president of the General Aviation Manufacturing Association (GAMA) and then CEO of Cessna Aircraft. I would work for Don Shepperd, sales manager, and was hired on a salaried plus commission basis.

A few words about Don Shepperd: he was an Air Force Academy graduate and a jet fighter pilot on temporary leave from Pan Am Airlines when he was hired as a sales manager for Grumman American. I had the privilege of working with him for almost two years until he returned to the military. Before his retirement, he became Brigadier General, overseeing all Air National Guard personnel nationwide. He was a brilliant young man, and I worked well with him and with much pleasure. We flew together many times, and I considered him a good friend.

After my initial training, I was given a brand new four-place 1973 Grumman American Traveler to perform my duties. It was a bright, all-yellow bird, and I enjoyed flying that airplane. I was to cover eleven North-Central states, demonstrate the airplane, establish new dealers, and attend any show that might fall in my territory. I made an appearance at the Oshkosh Airshow several times. I worked for Grumman American until 1978. During my stent with Grumman American, I built a dealer base from seven to about 25 dealers. I was the only Regional Manager to make quota in 1976. I logged over 2,500 hours during that time in a mix of models they built. However, I was transferred to Grumman AgCat (crop sprayer) division in 1974 as a temporary position. It was due to the shortage of gasoline nationwide and a general slowdown in sales.

I was to do this until 1975 when I returned to my original Regional Manager position. During that interim period, I worked out of Elmira, New York, where the AgCat was built. I was to call on all our national distributors and major aircraft users and participate in all state and national shows. I was mostly a Public Relations man; at that time, sales were a matter of taking orders. We were always sold out of spray planes. I used a Grumman American Traveler to visit my distributors from coast to coast.

When Tony was out of school, he would accompany me on many trips to California, Washington, and the southeastern states during this period. I always let him fly from the left seat, and he logged over 100 hours. Tony was too young to solo but became quite proficient at being a pilot. I enjoyed the company, and I'm sure he had a good time, also.

In 1976, Grumman moved its manufacturing facility to Savannah, Georgia. It is where the famous G2 Gulfstream corporate jet was manufactured. I would work out of Savannah until I left the company in 1978. At that time, Grumman sold its general aviation business to Al Paulsen Enterprises. The word was out that he would soon discontinue manufacturing the little general aviation airplanes and concentrate on the Gulfstream sales. The change resulted in my seeking employment with Bellanca Aircraft of Alexandria, Minnesota.

Bellanca Aircraft Company

Bellanca Aircraft Company hired me in late 1978. The only available territories were California, Arizona, Oregon, Washington, Idaho, Nevada, and Utah. I accepted the job and was given permission to fly home at least every two weeks, commercially or in the Viking. The pay was better, and I was given the use of a new Viking 300 for my demonstrator. It was a fast, modern, retractable, geared airplane that was a delight to fly. Probably one of my all-time favorites, not probably, but possibly.

My responsibilities were like they were with Grumman. There were more activities on the West Coast, and I needed to participate in more aviation events. For example, if I were in Salt Lake City on Friday, I would usually fly the Viking home. But if I were anywhere else and if the weather was marginal, I flew commercial. I established several new dealers and had one sale that consisted of five new airplanes at once. I helped that dealer by returning to Alexandria and ferrying one of his airplanes back, along with my dealer and another pilot. We flew loose formation all the way back to California. It was a fun trip.

Being gone so much strained my family relationship, so in 1979 we decided to sell our home in Schuyler and move to Paso Robles, California. It is about midway between Los Angeles and San Francisco—a delightful small town near the coast with a population of 25,000. We bought a new ranch-style home there, and I flew from the lovely local airport. Tony was out of high school by then, and Judy was married, so Gina was the only one we had with us at home. I'm sure it wasn't easy for Gina to make the move—like when I moved to California when I was 14. JoAnn went to work in the local hospital as a medical records technician.

Tony drove our Chrysler auto out to us along with his friend Fred. We flew back to Nebraska in the Viking. I let Tony fly from the left seat all the way. His friend Fred got terribly airsick enroute, and he wanted to take the bus home from Salt Lake City. I convinced him to take a bunch of Dramamine, and he slept in the backseat most of the way home. I wonder if he has been in a small airplane since. Things were going poorly for Bellanca, and I knew they were in financial straits when I moved to California. However, I thought my chances of finding employment would be better out there than they would have been in Nebraska. Bellanca paid for our move to the west coast, which helped financially.

San Luis Obispo And Apollo Aircraft

When my job with Bellanca was terminated, I began working for an FBO Apollo Aircraft in San Luis Obispo. It was located about 30 miles from Paso Robles. I was employed by a large Piper Aircraft dealer who operated at the Santa Barbara Airport. In addition, I would give a little dual instruction to keep myself current. I was salaried and worked on commission. I flew commercially to Vero Beach, Florida, and picked up one of the very first Piper Saratoga for our operation. I sold it retail later, possibly the first one sold on the west coast.

Back To Kansas City

In early 1980, I was contracted by Louis Kalman of KCH Inc. in Olathe, Kansas. He offered me a job in his large, well-organized operation. I knew him as he was one of my dealers when I worked for Grumman American. I accepted the job, and we made plans to return to the Midwest.

The house in California sold, and we drove to Paola, Kansas, where we purchased a new home. Paola was a small town about 35 miles south of Olathe, where I was to work. En route, Tony and Gina, driving our Dodge Colt, followed us in the Buick. They were rear-ended by a semi-tractor trailer on Interstate 80 shortly after we left Rock Springs, Wyoming. The car was totaled, but miraculously neither Tony nor Gina was seriously injured or killed. I carried a pistol in the car, and if Tony or Gina were killed, I would have shot the female truck driver. No question.

We returned to Rock Springs to the hospital until the two were released and then stayed overnight. After all their belongings were retrieved from the wrecked car, we put them in the Buick and continued. JoAnn was hired as Medical Records Director in Paola, and Gina started high school. After graduation, she enrolled at Emporia State College in Kansas.

My duties for KCH were sales, and I was made assistant chief flight instructor. We were a Cessna dealer with over 30 airplanes to teach in, sell, and lease. We were also a charter operation. I would fly instruction, airplane check-outs, photo flights, and be involved in the sales of new and used aircraft. Louis also gave me some helicopter flight instruction at that time. It was a busy place. However, Louis sold out later in 1980, and I went to work across the field for Kansas City Piper.

Kansas City Piper

Michelle Stauffer hired me as department sales manager. She was formally a salesperson for KCH and a good acquaintance of mine. I was also to give check-outs and occasional dual instruction. KC Piper was a Piper distributor, so I worked with other dealers in our territory. I also ferried and picked up aircraft for them. While I was working there, I found an opportunity to work for Eagle Aircraft Company. The headquarters was in Boise, Idaho, but they had contracted my old company, Bellanca, to build the crop sprayers in Alexandria, Minnesota. My earlier experience as a crop duster was paying off. I had prior acquaintances with many principals from my Bellanca and Grumman AgCat days.

Eagle Aircraft Corporation

I attended the National Aerial Application convention in Las Vegas and met with the executives associated with the Eagle Aircraft Corporation. They had their prototype crop sprayer on display, which impressed me. It was a beautiful white bi-plane with an exceptional 53-foot wingspan. I was offered a position with them and arranged to fly to Boise for indoctrination. I was then going to Alexandria, Minnesota, to fly the airplane. I acquainted myself with its construction and met with all the engineers and employees at the manufacturing plant. It was a brand-new facility manned by many of the former Bellanca employees. It was similarly constructed to the wonderful Viking, with wood, steel, and fabric. After accomplishing everything I was to do there, I flew a demonstrator airplane to Olathe, Kansas, where it was to be based. I continued to live in Paola.

My area of responsibility was all states east of the Mississippi River. This was almost half of the United States. I was to fly the Eagle to the operator's strip and demonstrate the airplane. Following a cockpit check-out, we let anyone fly it that so desired. I would fill up the spray plane with water to simulate a load. In all my experiences with doing that, I never had anyone so much as scratch an airplane. A tribute to its fine flying characteristics. It did have a huge 53-foot wind wingspan, so care had to be taken while taxiing on the ground. I landed at all types of fields, characteristic of crop spraying operations. In the event of an engine failure in flight, I probably wouldn't have chosen some of those fields to land on. It challenged my flying skill, as well, because if I couldn't land on their strips, I wouldn't be seen as much of a pilot. Plaid shirts, jeans, and boots were my business outfit.

These pilots, as a rule, are very talented. I still believe that crop sprayers are the best stick and rudder and fly by the seat of their pants pilots in aviation. I didn't say the smartest or greatest businessman, just the best pilots. I would fly up the Atlantic coast from Miami to Jacksonville at about 300 feet and just offshore, enjoying the scenery. I made a special effort to avoid the frequent kite flyers that are found on the beaches. It was flying at its best.

After one year or so, I picked up the company Bellanca Viking in Texas for personal use. I no longer had to fly the sprayer back and forth to Kansas—a very arduous and sometimes hazardous flight. I did continue to use the Eagle for all flights in the southeast since my Eagle was in Georgia. Once again, the sprayers had minimum instruments and no radios. It was a single-place airplane, with barely room for my flight charts. I carried my suitcase, briefcase, and whatever else I had in the front hopper.

One brief encounter was with law enforcement one night while landing in Deland, Florida. After shutting down the airplane on the ramp, the policeman pulled his car directly in front of my plane. It was a time when drug hauling by airplane, particularly crop sprayers, was prevalent. When I deplaned and pulled my suitcase out of the hopper, I began to give him a sales pitch on the attributes of the airplane. At first, he looked quizzical, then he smiled, told me to have a nice day, and drove off. The hopper was designed to carry the chemical, but I didn't use it, so it was clean. It made an excellent trunk. The Viking, by comparison, was a comfortable four-place, high-speed airplane that I could fly from Olathe to Georgia in three or four hours nonstop. I kept an Eagle in Olathe and one in Americus, Georgia, so my demonstrator was already there when I flew to Georgia. I still covered many miles with the Eagles, but the long trip back and forth to Kansas was much more manageable.

I established the FBO in Americus, Georgia, as a sales and service center for the Eagle. Consequently, I spent a lot of time there and made some very good friends I would later reconnect with. We based several Eagles there for possible sales or leases.

In 1983, the folks in Americus and I came up with the brilliant idea of putting on the first-ever crop spraying competition event held in the United States. I talked the company into furnishing the aircraft, of which we already had five, and putting on a so-called "Dog and Pony show" on a national scale. After much work and planning, the event took place in April 1983. We had national press and were on ABC late-night news. It would be excellent exposure for our newly designed airplane. It was, and my superiors agreed.

The event, a three-day affair, went off with no particular problems. None of the competitors had any experience in flying the Eagle, so they were all on even footing. The participants came from all over the country and were chosen after being given written and oral exams. There were 35 competitors, all going after the cash prize. I believe it was $5,000 or so. They had all expenses paid and would arrive three days in advance for us to advise them on the curriculum and let them fly the Eagle. My job was to give a cockpit check-out to each contestant and verify that they knew the airplane's capabilities and control layout. That was a lot of detailed work. I think I damaged my knees during that time, jumping off the wing and hitting the ground flat-footed. Over and over. I jumped off the wing onto the asphalt. There needed to be a step to assist me.

The show went off as planned, and we were lucky enough to have celebrities like John Glenn, Jimmy Carter, and his brother Billy. Bob Hoover was hired to give an outstanding air show in the P-51 Mustang and his Twin Aero Commander. We also paid for many other famous air show pilots. Grandstands were erected, booths were set up, a sound system was activated, and the show was on. We charged a respectable admission.

Once again, as a tribute to the Eagle, we had no accidents or incidents during those days. I'm sure the owners of the company held their breath. We all stayed at the Holiday Inn, and every night was party time. One of the co-sponsors was Miller High Life beer. Needless to say, there was no shortage of beer. It was a time to remember, and I don't think there will ever be another event like this. I met so many great people, competitors, and helpers that I'm sure I couldn't name them all. It was a real team effort, and we were proud of everyone that contributed.

Unfortunately, Eagle was in its death throws. The economy for the farmers could have been better, hence less money for spraying. We were trying to sell a $100,000 airplane to operators that could barely afford a used $20,000 Cessna or Piper. And there were still plenty of those around.

The Eagle would outperform all of them, but the cash flow didn't make sense to the operators. Eagle would go out of business shortly, and the remaining unsold airplanes would be deeply discounted by up to 50 percent. I sold out of my home in Paola for a while, but the handwriting was on the wall. I would be seeking another job.

Back In Paola

This period in my life was not very rewarding. I continued to search for aviation-related employment. During the 1980s, the aviation business as a whole was in the doldrums. Product liability soared for the manufacturers to as much as $30,000 per airplane. I knew I could return to KCH, as Louis had bought the operation back, but I no longer wanted that type of life. Unless I had to, which I later did.

I was hired by Florafax, a flowers-by-wire organization similar to FTD, based in Tulsa, Oklahoma. Once again, I was driving all over and making cold calls to florists. I thought I left that business long ago. I was not happy. I did that for a very short time. Then I was hired by the local car dealership. We sold Chevrolets, Oldsmobile, Pontiacs, and Buicks. My employers were very fine people, and I enjoyed the relationship, but that wasn't what I really wanted to do. I called up a previous acquaintance who had been a representative for Cessna Ag planes. I read that he was president of Helio Aircraft in Pittsburg, Kansas. He asked that I come down for an interview. Pittsburg is about 90 miles south of Paola. I drove down, and he promptly hired me as sales manager. The airplane manufacturing plant was in Pittsburg, having been moved from the east coast. It was a short takeoff and landing airplane Air America and the CIA used in Vietnam. I was very excited. Once again, I would do what I did best—strapping an airplane on my rear and taking off.

Helio Aircraft Company

In April 1984, I began working for Helio Aircraft Company as a sales manager. I would drive to Pittsburg, Kansas, on Mondays, spend the week there, then come home for the weekend. The Helio was a world-famous, 6-place, single-engine airplane, with exceptional performance, especially during takeoffs and landings. It had been built for many years in the New England area but was now manufactured in Kansas by a group of venture investors.

After my flight check-out and familiarization, I flew the Helio to Florida to demonstrate it to several interested parties. I accomplished this but did not generate any sales. One of the problems was that this type of airplane was more suited to Third World countries, most places with short, unimproved airports. Missionaries and the like used them. Here in the United States, we had an abundance of airports, but most of them were adequate for most manufactured airplanes being built here. While it was a fine airplane, there just wasn't much market for them. We designed a crop sprayer using Helio's delicate wing design but never passed the prototype stage.

The plan was to fly the Helio Courier to Bolivia, South America, and demonstrate it to the Bolivian Army during an

Army Day celebration in May. My co-pilot was a young man who had ferried many airplanes to South America for Cessna and had extensive experience making ferry flights of that nature. We were to fly to Florida, then across the Caribbean to Puerto Rico, where we planned to stay overnight. Then the flight was to continue over the Gulf of Mexico to Venezuela. From Venezuela, we planned to cut across the Brazilian jungles, up the backside of the Andes mountains, and on to LaPaz, Bolivia.

However, during the flight leg to Puerto Rico, we encountered some problems. Flying in the dark, over the ocean, at 13,000 feet, the motor acted up and began sporadically quitting. We were 57 nautical miles from Puerto Rico and could see the city's lights on the horizon. It became apparent that we may not be able to make it to San Juan. We declared an emergency and were directed to the nearest landing facility in Arecibo. We made it, but that was the most extended, most tense situation I had ever experienced, and I had a bunch. We were not equipped for night water ditching, and our chances of survival would have been minimal.

The next day, the local mechanics could not ascertain the intermittent cause of the fuel starvation. It was a newly designed engine installation, and perhaps all the bugs still needed to be worked out. Also, it might have happened because of the extended flight time at high altitudes and low temperatures. I was less than enthusiastic about continuing, and we had yet to discover the cause of the engine issues. I called home and told JoAnn and Gina the situation. I remember Gina saying, "Dad, forget the trip and just come home." For once, I did as told. I caught a commercial flight and returned to the States. My co-pilot continued, and he made it as far as I knew. I was concerned with the flight over the vast jungles and tall mountains. We might not have been so lucky if we experienced the same engine problem again. As it turned out, we were already behind schedule and would have missed the demonstration for the Bolivian Army Show anyway.

When I arrived back in Pittsburg, what basically had happened in my short absence, I was totally blindsided. The business went into receivership and closed. I demonstrated the Helio to some prospective buyers of the company in Tulsa and ran a few more errands. I flew a new Cessna spray plane that was being used by engineering to Greenwood, Mississippi. The airplane's owner and part-owner of the business were concerned that it might have been attached to the legal action, as they owed so much money to the airport. A long-time acquaintance of mine asked me to sneak the Cessna out of there and return it to him. He flew me back to Pittsburg in his personal airplane, a twin Beechcraft. I was out of a job again. I felt fortunate to have the opportunity to fly and be involved with such a famous airplane as the Helio, but I had to forge ahead. I went back to work at KCH for Louis Kalman.

Return To KCH

I flew for Louis from July 1984 until March 1986. I kept very busy flight instructing, giving check-outs, and biennial flight reviews. One student would stand out particularly. It was Glenn Grupp, a German student whose father was an acquaintance of Louis's that lived in Tanzania, Africa. I helped teach Glenn through his private, commercial, and instrument ratings. Louis taught him for his helicopter rating. Glenn lived with Louis in Stanley, Kansas. We became very good friends, and during his cross-country training, we flew to Florida and back, and also to Los Angeles, Las Vegas, and back. He received some excellent instruction and had a good idea of what the United States was like. Not just Kansas and Missouri.

After he returned home, Glenn settled on the Island of Föhr in northern Germany. His fiancé had visited him in Kansas and accompanied us on the Florida trip. When they were to get married, he invited me to a wedding in Germany, which I attended. It was a wonderful experience, and I would very much like to visit someday. During this phase of my life, my marriage with JoAnn deteriorated to the point that she left me and moved to Lincoln to live with Judy. I'm sure my constant traveling and uncertainty of where and for whom I would work next didn't help. I think she would have preferred I had a local 8 to 5 job. There were times when I felt the same way, but it was my opinion that I didn't have the necessary skills to accomplish this. I had already dedicated so much of my life to aviation.

Gina was in college by then, and it was just the two of us in Paola. I put the house up for sale and started investigating where I might live. Preferably, it would be nearer to my work. I eventually bought a small house in Gardner Lake, Kansas. It was on the lake with a lovely boat dock. I continued to work for Louis and accumulated an additional 850 hours of flight time. In March 1986, I was approached by Rick Bailey to run a flight school at the Richards Gebauer Airport in Belton, Missouri. I accepted and would begin my new position there.

Richards Gebauer Airport

In March 1986, I began instructing at the Richards Gebauer Airport. Richards Gebauer was an ex-military airbase that was deactivated. All that remained were some National Guard Warthog attack airplanes with which we would share the airspace. I was appointed chief flight instructor. We mainly used Cessna 150 airplanes. I would accumulate an additional 250 hours and also teach at Johnson County Airport for Louis, as needed. I applied for the aircraft accident investigator position with the National Transportation Safety Board, which had a Kansas City, Missouri branch. I applied twice. At first, I was not hired, but when the position came open again, I reapplied. It was 1987, and I always felt I had the qualifications for the job.

I was interviewed at the Federal Building in downtown Kansas City. Shortly after, I was called by the NTSB Director on a Sunday night at home to tell me I was accepted. I would begin employment in June 1987. It was a federal job that was very much sought after, and the qualifications were very stringent. They wanted people with considerable general aviation experience, not necessarily airline or military pilots. My years of General Aviation experience had paid off.

National Transportation Safety Board

Sworn in on June 11, 1987, I immediately began learning my responsibilities. I was to investigate aircraft accidents and incidents and submit written reports. In addition, I was to formulate safety proposals dealing with General aviation. We covered all relevant aircraft events for eight states. All aircraft accidents in that territory were our responsibility. I would carry a badge. The NTSB is a relatively small group consisting of about 350 total employees. We had offices in ten locations in the Continental United States and Alaska. Headquarters was here in Washington D.C. Each office usually had less than ten employees. The staff typically comprised air safety investigators, railway accident investigators, and highway accident investigators. There were a total of 60 of us aircraft accident investigators. I would be on call 24 hours a day, seven days a week.

Shortly after being hired, I was sent to Oklahoma City to the FAA Academy for intensive, specialized training. We were taught everything from metallurgy, photography, investigative skills, and anything we might encounter during an investigation. As you might expect, an immense amount of paperwork was also involved. I also would go to Washington, D.C., for additional training from time to time. While traveling on official business, anywhere, I would ride jumpseat in the cockpit with the pilots of commercial flights. We always had priority if it were business-related. We were constantly being trained for any situation that might arise. Of interest were any new aircraft models that had been introduced and any problems that might have arisen.

If we were to go to the scene of an accident, we would be the investigator in charge, referred to as the **TIC**. It meant we were completely in charge of everything that happened there. In addition, we would be in charge of all law-enforcement personnel and FAA personnel. We controlled and secured the entire scene, including TV reporters, lawyers, and insurance people.

A lot of coordination was required, and proper communication was vital. We would photograph the scene of the accident for documentation, plus take pictures and measurements of anything that might be germane to the investigation. Later we would check for any and all communications the pilot might have had with the flight controlling agencies. I would examine the pilot's credentials, ratings, flight physical history, and flight currency. If it were pertinent, we would check his flight routing and where he last refueled. The weather was also documented. We would contact the engine and airplane manufacturers, such as Cessna, Piper, or Beechcraft, so that they might assist with the investigation. Radios and autopilots were scrutinized to see if they might have been connected to the accident. Also, we would line up, question, and take statements from any available witness. In the case of fatal injuries, we would ascertain that the county coroner properly removed the body or bodies from the scene. We tried to leave no stone unturned to get to the truth and make our determination.

If recovered, an autopsy of the pilot in command was required in all fatal aircraft accidents. Plus, we would have the medical doctor remove key body parts, and tissues, to be sent to our laboratory in Oklahoma. This was to check for possible incapacitation of the pilot or the presence of drugs and alcohol. It was a very responsible position, and we were well-trained to perform as expected. Usually, we were the only NTSB person on the scene. Next, we would compile all the pertinent information we gathered and make our final report. It included all relevant paperwork, diagrams, photographs, and all information and documentation from the engine and aircraft manufacturers. This also would include contributing factors and probable cause. It would usually take up to six months to finalize the report. Headquarters in Washington would review our findings and either agree or disagree or possibly request additional information. Names of the pilots were never given. Only the date of the mishap, aircraft type, location, and aircraft registration number would comprise the official record.

We moved to a new facility in Lenexa, Kansas, in 1989, and was 20 miles closer to my home. Nothing else changed except our location. We were based in the vast federal building downtown. It was a challenging commute, especially during bad weather. That was the same year I earned the distinction of an **Outstanding Performance Award**.

In 1991, due to budget constraints, the headquarters in Washington decided to cut down on expenses and planned to close the Kansas City and Denver offices. My option was to join the NTSB office in Chicago. After extensive investigation on several trips, I decided I didn't want to move to Chicago. I would continue working in Kansas City until they officially closed that office.

I was the last one to leave the NTSB office in Kansas City. I was given office space for a few months at the FAA's general aviation district office located at the Kansas City International Airport. Along with many FAA employees, I was the only NTSB person working there. The commute was definitely much longer. But I met another bunch of great people and enjoyed the experience. I tried to switch to the FAA at the FAA's suggestion, but they were only hiring females and minorities at the time. I decided to retire early when it was time to terminate my Kansas City location.

My retirement in June 1992 couldn't have been more uneventful. I really didn't want to, but moving to Chicago was my only option, which I had already decided against. During my employment with the NTSB, I determined probable cause for nearly **600 aviation accidents** in five years. The list comprised any aircraft that had a registration number. It included airplanes, helicopters, homebuilt aircraft, crop sprayers, hot air balloons, and occasional air carriers, such as commuter airlines. We also had a major airline crash in Sioux City, Iowa, that made the national headlines.

Although working for the NTSB was a highlight of my career, it was also a very depressing job at times. Whenever the phone rang at work, it was because someone had some misfortune. It wasn't a fatality most of the time, but in any case, someone was not very happy. I wore a pager and was called on weekends and evenings, which substantially curtailed my activities. Your time, indeed, was not your own.

While employed with the NTSB, I was given special permission to continue flight instruction. I helped a couple more students attain their private pilot certificates, and hardly a week passed that I wasn't flying with someone. I felt this was an excellent way to stay in touch with general aviation and not get too far removed from the reality of real-world flying in general aviation. I owned a little Cessna 120 that I kept at the Gardener airport, so I'd fly it if I weren't teaching someone. I remarried in 1988 to Ruby. A former student of mine, she moved in with me at the Gardener Lake home. The marriage was traumatic, and looking back was a big mistake.

Reminiscing on my time with the NTSB, I could write a book on all the strange and bizarre occurrences that took place during those years. No one could imagine the situations that transpired and other scenarios that were harder yet to believe. I have a record of each accident, and reviewing them brings back vivid memories of what happened and why on that day. As usual, though, the majority of accidents of any kind are predominantly human errors. Always has been and always will be.

A word from the Editor
The Unsung Heros - "One cannot overstate John's impeccable work at the NTSB. As a pilot with a broad base of aviation experience, he had a unique investigative perspective. His proliferative efforts illustrated the common dire contrast between his life's work and human failures in the realm of aviation, a strange and stress-filled juxtaposition. A crash starts as a mystery, becomes a complex puzzle, and may evolve into an interrogation. Once all the facts are in (photographically documenting the on-site crash, situational reconstruction, weather, evaluating the ATC

tapes and the black box, studying the logbooks, the mechanical and maintenance history, interpersonal background, including the pilot's mental status, and of course, the autopsy report), the investigator becomes the judge and the author of his elaborate, traumatic report-a rewarding but challenging and demanding job. It is an uncompromised sifting through history to verify that the current case you are working on is not a new and innovative way to wreck an airplane."

Raven Aircraft Company, Americus, Georgia

Before my retirement, I talked to Frankie Williams of Americus, Georgia, who was now the Airport Manager. He was a very good friend and was one of the principals involved in putting on the crop dusting competition in 1983. Ruby and I flew to Florida in April to attend Fun and Sun in our little Yankee airplane. We stopped in Americus to stay overnight on the way to Florida. Frankie said he had established a company with some Germans, Raven Aircraft. It was for the purpose of importing ex-East German crop sprayers. These were left over after the Berlin Wall came down and East Germany was no longer a communist country. There were fleets of these Polish crop sprayers located all over East Germany, and they were no longer being used due to the communist loss of power. He wanted to know if I was interested in being a sales manager, and I told him yes. I would have to move to Americus, Georgia, to perform my duties.

In June 1992, Ruby and I began preparing for the move. We left our house at Gardener Lake, Kansas, completely furnished, and took only what personal items we could haul in our two cars, plus our cat. Raven Aircraft was to pay for a rental apartment, all utilities, and all new furnishings for us to live in. I was to have a salaried position with incentive commissions. Ruby was hired as my secretary and bookkeeper. We would have health insurance and only had a few personal expenses.

Raven Aircraft would import used crop sprayers from East Germany, which we would then put up for sale domestically and internationally. They would test-fly the airplanes in East Germany, disassemble them for shipment, put them in shipping containers, and ship them to Savannah, Georgia, a port of entry. We would have them trucked to Americus, where we would uncrate, reassemble, and prepare them for certification. We also accepted all the support equipment that came with the airplanes. We received each aircraft's engines, propellers, airframe parts, and documentation. Logs, records, and such. These parts filled a large warehouse, and some were stored outside. My office and Ruby's were located in the same warehouse. These were exciting times for the city of Americus, as this was a momentous occasion for them. We had an open house displaying all the types of airplanes we would sell. The Mayor and all the city officials, as were the owners from Germany, were present.

Airplanes began arriving with truckloads of parts. They were reassembled and tied down in rows on the ramp adjacent to the airport. We had almost 40 of the 600 horsepower Kruk models, three of the Zlin–37 trainers, and about a dozen of the 1,000 horsepower M–18 Dromediers. It became an impressive site as more and more aircraft arrived.

Quickly, we realized that we would need help from the German owners. They had previously shipped 40 airplanes to Venezuela by ocean transport. These did not require U.S.-type certificates. But they were unable to collect the money from their customers. Last I heard, they were still in the seaport, slowly rotting, rusting, and deteriorating in the original crates. Regardless the Germans thought that we should be able to sell them in lots of 40 or so, just as they did. The fact that they never collected any money for them and were out shipping costs should have been discussed. Ours was a very different market in which we would sell them one or two at a time, which we did.

Next, airplanes sold here in the U.S. must conform to the U.S.-type certificate. Only one model had the necessary type certificate, the M–18, and we only had about twelve. We needed to ensure all the decals, instrument markings, operation information, and other things were printed in English. Fortunate to have a former East German young man working for us. He could translate the paperwork. The FAA would then send someone down from Atlanta to see that everything was correct. We had to test-fly the airplane while he observed. If everything went well, it still took almost six months before we could certify and sell the airplane. We also had extreme pressure from the U.S. importers of that model of Airplane. They were selling new ones, and ours were used. Naturally, our selling prices were far below what they could charge for their airplanes, which was an apparent bargain. They tried to stop us in any way they could, including trying to influence the FAA from certifying them. We succeeded in what we started to do with much effort and even more communication.

In addition, the 40 Kruk model airplanes that were tied down did not have a U.S.-type certificate. We thought we might be able to accomplish this, and Frankie made several trips to the Polish factory in Warsaw to meet with the senior officials. I made one trip. We met the manufacturers and attempted to have them propose a type certificate, but all attempts failed. Even though thousands of dollars changed hands, they could see no reason to spend countless dollars to certify the Kruk when it was out of production. It had only been used by the Communist block countries.

My trip to Poland was a great experience. I was there for about one week, and after several daily meetings at the factory, we were treated to a tour of Poland. It was by company airplane and many buses. We went to Kraków, Bielsko, the Pope's birthplace, and Auschwitz, the Nazi Jewish concentration camp. I had an extra day, so I took a bus tour of Warsaw. It was a wonderful adventure. Everyone that I met there was gracious and kind. The Polish are a poor but very proud people. They had been through an awful lot during the war and occupations by the Russians. Today, the airplanes are still sitting on the field in Americus, where they were in 1992, also deteriorating. Engine propellers are U.S.-type certificates so we could sell those items, but not the airframe.

I sold several of the M-18s. In fact, the last three I sold were delivered to Australia. These were shipped directly from Germany to Australia. Needless to say, there was much paperwork involved in this transaction. We had to send one of our key aircraft mechanics over there so he could supervise the reassembly and prepare them for flight. However, the supply of that model, the M-18, in Germany had been used up, and more was needed. New ones were obtainable, but we were not a dealer, nor could we be. This took about two years to transpire, and the handwriting was again on the wall.

While in Americus, I was contacted by Larry Reineke of Central City, Nebraska, about some problems he had with the temporary airport management. The man who was acting manager turned out to be a felon. He was sent back to jail on drug-related charges and embezzlement. Larry was a resident crop sprayer in Central City and a long-time acquaintance. During our conversations, he thought I could be a likely candidate for Airport Manager in Central City. I wrote the City Manager, who said I could fill the position. We made plans to leave Americus, and I was to move to Central City to become the new Airport Manager. We loaded up our two vehicles and drove back to Gardener.

Return To Nebraska

We stopped over in Gardener to sell our property. After it closed, I went to Central City to begin my new job as Airport Manager. Ruby was to store some of the furniture, then come up to join me. She had a place to stay near Gardener. After arriving in Central City, I rented, what I thought, would be a temporary apartment until we purchased a home. My job started with cleaning the large hanger that would be mine at no charge. I brought my Yankee airplane there from the Grain Valley Airport outside of Kansas City, where it had been stored. My responsibility was for hangar rental, fuel supplies, and records, keeping the grounds, and all associated duties. I was salaried with all health benefits and soon started lessons in a Cessna 150. Dennis O'Nele brought in the plane, agreed to insure it, and let me use it for instruction. I had taught him to fly many years before. My mother Albina and Jim were together in the local nursing home, and I could see them regularly.

Larry asked me if I could help him spray crops shortly after arrival. I told him it had been at least 25 years since I sprayed, except for demonstration purposes, but I would give it a try. He took me to one of his hangars and said, "This is your plane." I was astounded to see it was one of the very same sprayer plane that I had picked up new in Afton, Wyoming, in 1967. In fact, it was the one I mentioned earlier that I had crashed and rebuilt. I got into the cockpit, which seemed to have shrunk, or I might have grown, started it up, and took off. A bit rusty, but no problem. The next day I was out spraying again. I was cautious because of my lack of recent experience, but we got along fine. Spraying paid very well and was a welcome addition to my salary. I could earn more than $1,000 a day when we were busy. We mostly sprayed as a two-airplane team. It worked great. The season would last until September. Then we would start again the next April or May.

Meanwhile, I began to look for a home. When I filled out a financial report to qualify for a loan, I discovered Ruby had depleted our savings, and I was deeply in debt. It was shortly after that she had divorce papers served on me. Ruby had never intended to accompany me to Central City. She had stored furniture that belonged to me in Kansas City, and I was to pay monthly rent until I sent for it. It was a bitter lesson for me, and I later discovered how much she had done with our finances.

Things became quiet around the airport after spray season. I became bored and missed the sales activity. So I applied for a job as a sales manager for Zenith Aircraft in Mexico, Missouri. I was given consideration, but the position would open in December. I returned to Olathe, Kansas, and worked as a salesman for the Piper dealer there until they were ready for me in Missouri. In December 1994, I reported to Zenith Aircraft Company for my new job.

Zenith Aircraft Company

Zenith aircraft company had been primarily an airplane home-build kit builder with its headquarters in Canada. They opened a branch in Mexico, Missouri, making parts for the kits they sold. I was to operate out of Mexico, and they would have a couple of CH–2000 experimental airplanes there. The planes I flew were still experimental with the Canadian registry as Homebuilt Aircraft. I was to fly nationwide to demonstrate and help determine the market for this two-place training aircraft. They planned to certify it with the FAA in the U.S. as soon as possible.

I rented an apartment in Mexico, Missouri, and immediately began my job. My first trip in December 1994 was to the southeast U.S., where the weather was more suitable. I demonstrated the airplane in Miami, Florida, and Georgia flight schools. The acceptance of the aircraft was lukewarm at best. It still had all the earmarks of a home-built aircraft. Once, after just taking off from Clearwater, the left cockpit door flew open and was torn completely off by the wind. It was a gull-wing door, and reaching and closing it in flight was impossible. My good fortune was that it did not hit the tail and make the airplane uncontrollable. The air temperature was in the low 40s and seasonably cold for Florida. The wind and severe turbulence made it impossible to read a chart, and I had difficulty even seeing and staying warm. I had an appointment in Ocala, Florida, to repair the radio, so I continued to Ocala instead of returning for a landing. I had to rely on my memory of former trips to navigate. I mostly followed interstate highways. It was a most miserable flight, lasting about one hour. I hit Ocala airport on the nose and gladly landed.

When queried, the Clearwater operator discovered they had recovered the faulty door. They said it miraculously had landed on a police car. A little levity there, but I wasn't in a humorous mood. I had them fly it to Ocala, where the local aircraft mechanics jerrybuilt it back on the airplane. From then on, I had to use the right-hand door to board the Zenith. I called the office, told him what had happened, and flew back to Mexico on another airplane. The sudden loss of the door was a frightening and dangerous experience. It could have taken the tail off and caused a catastrophic crash. In an article on the test airplane in AOPA magazine, they implied that it was not a big deal. They also said that the pilot opened the door in flight to take a picture, which caused the door to fail. That is absolutely not true. I should know.

I attended the Sun and Fun show in Lakeland, Florida, in April 1995. I hoped to set up a display there. The president flew down a new and improved model from Canada for me to demonstrate during the five-day show. I flew with numerous individuals, mostly aviation publication writers and editors. I also flew a tight formation for air-to-air photos. The way Zenith handled that was a bit scary. Most of the flights went well except for a couple of foreign writers with communication problems.

The highlight of being at the Sun and Fun Aviators show was where I met my wife-to-be, Elva Pierce. She was tending the exhibit for *Flight Training* magazine, and I stopped by to see an old acquaintance who worked for the magazine. I visited the booth on several occasions. During these stops, I began to get acquainted with Elva. I'm still trying to determine if I met my friend Loy Hickman, but my interest made a new turn. I learned she was a widow and lived in Parkville, Missouri. Elva was a business manager and part-owner of the popular magazine *Flight Training*. I asked her if I might take her out for dinner when I was in the area. She said she thought that would be OK, and of course, I made it evident that I would be there as soon as I could arrange it. I did, and we went out for lunch. The rest is history.

Following the show, I remained in Lakeland. I had an appointment with Bill Kelly, ex-Piper test pilot, who now worked for *Aviation Consumer* magazine. We were to spend almost two days flying the airplane, judging its qualities, or in this case, lack of them. After the magazine published the test, it was the worst test flight article I have ever read. Unless many improvements were made to the airplane, soon, it would almost be unmarketable. As far as I was concerned, this was the last straw. I called the City Manager in Central City for possible reemployment with a higher salary this time. He was receptive. I would be moving there soon. Again.

Back To Central City

I returned to Central City in 1995, and this time, Larry Reineke had purchased a house trailer which he put alongside the main hanger where I would reside. There was no rent to pay this time. It was early May, and crop spraying activity had not started yet. I made a trip or two to Parkville, Missouri, and on each occasion, Elva and I would go out for dinner. We seemed entirely compatible, and I wished I wasn't living so far away.

Then I received a phone call from a friend in Olathe, whom I taught to fly. I had told Vic Phillips to watch the papers and if the Gardener airport ever came up for grabs, to call me. He did, and I flew to Gardener to meet with the manager. After a brief interview, it was agreed that I could be the airport fixed-base operator and live on the premises. There was no compensation or salary, but the airport had great potential. And living there, utility costs are free as compensation. I gave notice to the City of Central City and made plans to move to Gardner, Kansas.

Gardner Aviation

June 1995. My first objective was to lease some airplanes I could use for teaching. I still had my Yankee, but it could have been better for beginning students. Because I was well acquainted with the general area from previous employment, I could line up three airplanes on leaseback. They would be two Cessna 150s and one Cessna 172. These aircraft would suffice, and I would have access to other planes based there. Plus, I still had my Yankee for personal trips. My student base immediately began to grow, and I was swamped most all the time. I accumulated almost 1,000 initial flight hours, primarily dual instruction. I did many biennial flight reviews and check-outs.

My divorce from Ruby was finalized, and she got more than I thought she should. I was glad to be out of the marriage. I was seeing Elva practically every weekend by then. We also went to Bella Vista, Arkansas, several times. We made trips to Washington D.C. to visit her son, and during the summer of 1997, I flew to the Outer Banks in North Carolina to enjoy a few days on the seashore with Elva and her family. I felt a promising future was in store for the two of us and thought marriage would be in order. We were married on December 27, 1997, in an Episcopal church in Parkville. I moved into her home at Riss Lake, Parkville, but continued to commute to Gardner during the week. In September 1998, I sold the Gardener business. I accompanied Elva on several trade show trips, such as Los Angeles, New Orleans, and Las Vegas. She had many responsibilities at these trade shows, and I kept her company. I greatly enjoyed it and renewed some old acquaintances on some of those trips.

Parkville Flying Service

In February 2000, I started a one-man, one-airplane flight school at Noah's Ark Airport near Parkville, Missouri. I purchased a Cessna 150 from a friend and accumulated a small group of students. I flew an additional 75 hours before we took the plane to our new home in Houston, Maryland, in September 2000.

Easton Maryland

We moved to and retired in Easton, Maryland. A small town of about 13,000, located on the Delmarva Peninsula across from the Chesapeake Bay: we lived in a controlled community called the Easton Club. We had a golf club, tennis courts, a swimming pool, croquet grounds, and a nice restaurant. We were located on the Tred Avon Estuary. Many homes, including ours, had a pier on the water. The Tred Avon connects with the Chesapeake Bay. Theoretically, we could sail from our dock and go around the world. Not likely in our little boat.

It's a beautiful location, with a milder climate than we had been used to. Wildlife was abundant there: Eagles, Osprey, herons, ducks, geese, egrets, hummingbirds, songbirds, and of course, turkey vultures. We are on the Eastern Migratory Path for geese, and they winter here by the thousands. Also, deer and foxes are found locally, along with squirrels and groundhogs. All are seen in our backyard. The deer were far from the nuisance they were in Parkville. Easton was voted one of the top 10 small towns in the nation and has a very intriguing history, going back to having the oldest active church in the United States. It is a Friends Church that originated in 1680. Being one of the original 13 Colonies, Maryland has a great historical background. The town has all the necessary amenities with excellent medical facilities. With its brick sidewalks and old buildings, the original downtown has significant attractions with all its quaint shops and art galleries. Restaurants abound, from fast food to much higher class and ethnic restaurants. Almost everything is within walking distance, a far cry from driving all over Kansas City to accomplish something. They also have an excellent airport here with all the necessary facilities. Many corporate jets are based here, along with elite jet sales organizations.

We also have a marina, where you can launch your boat or base it in a slip. The marina is also a port for commercial fishermen. It is rural here, with farming still being a prevalent occupation. The speed limits on our excellent roads are 50 and 55 mph. However, we are only about an hour and a half from Baltimore or Washington, D.C. The Atlantic Ocean and its excellent beaches are about the same distance.

The little Cessna was used to give rides, as it was much easier to see the sites from the air than in a car. Our County has over 600 miles of shoreline. However, I sold the airplane after the 911 occurrence as it became somewhat restrictive to fly around here because we were so near the U.S. Capitol. I still dabble in aviation, but not to the extent I would like. I have a current flight instructor rating but have let my physical expire. Elva is very much involved in volunteer activities, mainly with the hospital auxiliary and the church. I live the life of a retired man keeping my little dog Midnight a Schipperke company.

Synopsis

I could write pages and pages about my flying experiences, but I will only write about some of the situations that I believe might be of interest. As I look through all my logbooks and over 12,600 hours of flight time, it brings many memories: some good, some bad, some funny, and some not so amusing. I'll first write about emergencies I've had while flying.

As near as I can remember, according to my logs, I have had at least eight forced landings, some immediate, some deferred, plus one wreck. The crash occurred when I was spraying, and I had mentioned it earlier (in the Crop Spraying chapter). I described my first forced landing during my early flying lessons. The time my engine failed was during my first lesson with Amos Bankson. I have previously mentioned several of the others, but one stands out.

Working for Bellanca, I was based on the West Coast. I flew back to Alexandria, Minnesota, through Nebraska. Then I was to fly to our annual summer company picnic. I had picked up a friend in Phoenix and dropped him off in Grand Island. I stayed at home for the weekend. Then on Monday, I flew with JoAnn and Gina to Alexandria for the picnic and festivities, which lasted about three days. We returned to Nebraska, and the following day, I planned to fly to Grand Island, about 60 miles, to pick up my friend, take him back to Phoenix, and continue to California.

It was a beautiful summer morning when I left Columbus, so I flew lower than usual to admire the scenery. My course to Grand Island would take me directly over the Central City Airport. As I approached the airport, at about 500 feet of altitude, I turned a little to the right to not go directly over the field, as I could see better. It was spray season, so I wanted to see if there was any activity on the airfield. When I was about 1/2 mile from the airport, the engine sputtered and began to quit. Then it stopped dead. The prop was frozen in space, a very unnatural occurrence. I was on the base leg for a landing, so I lowered the landing gear, applied some flaps, and landed at the Central City airport. It was almost a routine landing. Except for one thing, my engine had just failed.

After I coasted clear of the runway, I told the mechanic what happened, then called my sister to come and get me. From her house, I phoned the Grand Island airport to tell my friend he better catch an airliner because I couldn't make it there. In retrospect, had the engine quit even 30 seconds sooner or 30 seconds later, I would not have been in a position to land at the airport. Had it stopped an hour or two before, it might've been much worse on our way home from Alexandria. And, had it run another hour or two, it might have happened over the New Mexico mountains or at night, which would be a much worse scenario, quickly fatal. It certainly wasn't because of any skill or planning on my part. There may be a reason for what happens and when. As the saying goes, maybe my number wasn't up.

I knew the engine was having problems, even when I was in California. It began to use oil more than before, turning black and sooty. After the engine was torn down and examined, it was discovered that a piston failed because of a broken ring. I learned that when a machine tries to tell you something, listen.

Previously, I mentioned the deferred force landing in Puerto Rico. That differed from the above case as about 20 or 30 minutes transpired before landing. There was a lot of time to ponder what might happen. But it was over in the forced landing in Nebraska, maybe in 30 seconds. Not much time to think and worry. While spraying, I blew a crankshaft seal shortly after takeoff, which resulted in oil drenching the windshield. So much that I could only see out the sides of the plane; I was able to land immediately before the engine ran out of oil and seized. I would have had to make an off-airport forced landing a little further away from the airport. With what results, I wouldn't know. The engine lost a cylinder while on a training cross-country flight at night. It only had four to start. When we were about five miles from our destination airport, I declared an emergency with the Control Tower. Fortunately, we had enough altitude and power to make a safe landing.

Teaching

The saying goes, "If you want to learn all you can about something, teach." Looking back at all the pilots I flew with over 40 years of instruction. There would be no way of including those experiences here. Each person was a unique challenge. I always had to deal with their fears and perceived notions of right and wrong about flying. Gaining the student's trust and confidence was necessary. I understood their motivation. Why did they want to fly? To impress their friends, to use in their business, or were they going to make a career in aviation? The list goes on and on. I taught them all teenagers through senior citizens. Men and women. I never lost a student, nor had one injured, due to a flying accident. I taught over 130 students to completion of their private pilot's license. I did not have a student fail a checkride in over two decades.

Looking back through my logbooks, I could relate an interesting story about each of them. Of course, some were much better than others, but isn't that life? Some become professional airline pilots, military pilots, crop dusters, and instructors. In addition to the students I taught, I checked out many pilots in different aircraft I had never flown before in many cases. I taught aerobatics which appealed to some pilots but not everyone. I gave countless flight reviews to pilots, usually in their airplanes. I flew charters many times with occasional hesitant nervous passengers that might have been on their first airplane ride. I worked at airshows and gave rides to hundreds of people. I took them all: big, tiny, short, fat, and tall. I also specialized in tailwheel check-outs and crop spraying training. When I was in sales, I demonstrated the airplanes, then made the pilot look like an expert when he flew the aircraft to accomplish sales. I ferried airplanes, new and old, for repositioning. I flew bodies and injured people to their destinations. I even did aerobatic shows for compensation. I traveled with thousands of people through the years. My cup runneth over, indeed.

Lost Acquaintances

While working as a Regional Manager for Grumman American, I began listing all the people I knew who died in aircraft accidents. These were dealers, pilots who worked for dealers, instructors, acquaintances, people I knew well, and some I barely knew. When my count reached 57 fatalities, I quit keeping track. That was in 1975. It became too depressing.

One must realize that I was covering a large territory in my travels, and had I not been doing that, I might only know a few of them. I still think of flying as safe. I know that can be and must be treated with the utmost respect. One must be completely aware of your capabilities at all times. Know your equipment and plan your flight well. Always keep the back door open if you have to make a 180° turn. Don't be swayed by "Having to get there" unless you fully understand and can deal with the challenges you might encounter. Don't let your ego play any part in your decision. The ego probably doesn't know the first thing about flying anyway. Aviation can be safe and pleasurable as any means of transportation. But, it is very unforgiving if you abuse it. It is much more hard-hearted than surface and water transportation. You can't get out and walk in an airplane. If you did, the first step would be a dandy.

Miscellaneous Ramblings On Flight

Since the beginning of man on Earth, I'm sure that as he gazed into the sky and saw birds soaring, he envied them and likely wished he could do the same. It would be hundreds, maybe thousands, of years before he would even begin to attain flight. In the 1800s, maybe before, the early attempts were made in hot air balloons. They would go up. They would come down—no more, no less. Only the wind's direction and ability to supply hot air would determine their landing site. Or crash. Then came gliders. They would not go up but only down to their landing site. Or crash. But with the glider, the discovery of wings and generating lift were no longer a secret.

It was when the refined internal combustion engine used a propeller that generated thrust. By pulling the airplane forward, the relative wind was the result, hence providing lift from the aerodynamic shape of the wings. Man was now entering the age of flight in just over 100 years. It is a tiny fraction of the human occupancy of our planet. We have progressed from the Wright Brothers' first flight to supersonic jets, outer space travel, and satellites. How fortunate we are to have mastered this phenomenon.

From my personal experience, how would I describe the miracle of flight? The engine's roar on takeoff, the acceleration, and rolling of the wheels, then the flight controls come to life, followed by a lunge into the air. Every takeoff is different and unique. It would always be a thrill, accomplished by a rush of adrenaline. Landings also, but two factors usually accompany them. A letdown of emotions because the flight had ended and the gratification of a successful landing. If, indeed, it was. Once in flight, we would slip away from the surly bonds of Earth. Then comes the slow shrinking of the size of all viewed below as we gain altitude. How neat and clean it suddenly became. There was no trash along the roads or junkyards; everything would begin to look orderly and unsullied. There is no sensation of speed, just a slow passing of the scenery below.

How else could you view the migrating whales in the Pacific, except while flying low, slightly offshore? How else would you consider the orderly patchwork of section lines dotted with farms in rural America? How else could you view the Grand Canyon directly above or fly down into the canyons? How else could you rise above the clouds, discovering a bright sunny day above while it would still be dark and dreary below the clouds on Earth? How else could you view the stifling congestion on the interstate in large metropolitan areas as in Los Angeles? Pity those below, staring through their windshields, dodging traffic, jockeying for a position to exit, and trying to communicate on their cell phones. There are no traffic jams up here, no actual speed limits for little airplanes, no tailgating by inconsiderate drivers, no speed radars, no stoplights or stop signs, no right side of the road to stay on, no blinding headlights at night, no icy or snow-packed roads, and certainly no road rage— only the occasional call to or from ATC.

I would best describe the small airplane as one's personal flying carpet. Much as described in the *1001 Arabian Nights* novel of old. We fly over the fences, trees, and roads. We cross the rivers, lakes, and seas and fly over and around the mountains as if they didn't exist. We now see the Earth below as the eagle does. Isn't this what man has always desired for so many years? Aren't we the most fortunate generation ever? I think so.

All in all, my life has been a real trip. I wouldn't trade my experiences with anyone, but in retrospect, I doubt if anyone else would change for mine. I might have done some things differently, but given the circumstances at the time, I probably wouldn't have. Anyway, we can't change history. We must not dwell on what would've, could've, and should've been. We can only learn from our life experiences and perhaps pass on what we have learned. Try not to repeat mistakes, and use that knowledge to pursue happiness. Life goes on.

Dan Tyler's Master Pilot Award
Randy Lippincott photographer

Epilogue—Recollections Of Johnny Hruban

In reflecting on the fifty-plus years since my first flight lesson with John Hruban, I realize how large an influence his mentorship had on me in a very short time. Although I had flown frequently with my Dad, my first official flight lesson with Johnny was on February 1, 1970. At fifteen years of age, I had set the goal of my first solo flight on my sixteenth birthday, the youngest age allowed by FAA regulations. Seven flight lessons and twenty-three days later, Johnny flew with me for a few touch-and-go landings at the Central City airport and then asked me to taxi to the ramp. Exiting the airplane, he directed me to make three takeoffs and landings alone. Although I was a skinny kid, Johnny was a good-sized man and took up about two-thirds of the cockpit of N3085J, a small two-seat Cessna 150 aircraft. I recall how empty that right seat looked as I taxied for takeoff, and it felt like the aircraft leaped into the air, absent his two hundred-plus pounds of weight.

Following my initial solo, Johnny acquired a Citabria aircraft with aerobatic capability. Although stunt flight would not normally be part of pilot training at this early stage, five training flights with Johnny in his aerobatic aircraft proved an opportunity to fly the plane in flight attitudes that were neither safe nor legal in a more traditional flight trainer. In aviation parlance, Johnny taught me fundamental "stick and rudder" skills at the extremes of the aircraft's capability.

The runway paving project at the Central City airport forced Johnny to seek other employment. It brought our student/instructor relationship to an end after only nine months of training and about twenty hours of instruction received. He facilitated my continued flying from the Columbus airport, and we remained in occasional contact throughout the years, but we never flew together again.

I consider John Hruban an aviator to the core. In reading his story, his passion for flight is front and center. At what would occasionally be great personal cost, Johnny followed his dream across the United States. Evidence of the depth and breadth of his experience is seen in his selection as an Accident Investigator for the National Transportation Safety Board in 1987 and being awarded the Wright Brothers Master Pilot Award in 2013.

In FAA jargon, The Wright Brother's "Master Pilot Award" is the most prestigious the FAA issues to pilots certified under Title 14 of the Code of Federal Regulations (14 CFR) part 61. This award is named after the Wright brothers, the first U.S. pilots, to recognize individuals who have exhibited professionalism, skill, and aviation expertise for at least 50 continuous years while piloting aircraft as "Master Pilots." As a testimony to Johnny's mentorship of aviators, three of his students from the Central City area earned the FAA Master Pilot Award themselves.

My professional career included serving as a flight crew member on eleven different types of jet airliners and twenty-eight thousand hours of flight. As flight technology progressed, the aircraft that I flew became more and more automated, with my final years utilizing "fly-by-wire" technology, where a computer was the link between the pilot and the aircraft.

I now find myself on a retrospective journey in aviation. After retirement, I purchased a 1964 Piper Cherokee, very similar to the aircraft that Johnny conducted some of my flight lessons in 1970. I have taken great satisfaction in making several flights from my home in California to the Central City Airport. I have also noticed, over the years the constant use of flight automation has allowed my "stick and rudder" skills to atrophy. To embrace the joy of flight again, I need a few more lessons on the fundamentals from John Hruban, for he was a true master of the art of flying.

—Brian W. Tyler, Master Pilot

Photo Brian Tyler
Johnny endorsed Brian Tyler's student
license after his solo flight

Brian Tyler's Master Pilot Award
Randy Lippincott photographer

John and Albina Hruban, 1931

Editor Randy Lippincott's Biography

Randy Lippincott was born and raised on a farm in Nebraska. He attended a one-room country school and trained as a Special Forces combat medic in the Army during the Vietnam era. Randy started skydiving in 1969 at the Lincoln Sport Parachute Club in Lincoln, Nebraska, while attending Wesleyan. He made nearly 1,000 free falls (demonstration and competition) in Europe while serving with the 7th Army Parachute Team from 1971-72. It meant traveling every week throughout free Europe and behind the Iron Curtain. They wintered in Aviano, Italy, to practice without interruption.

Lippincott began flying when he was 16 and earned the Wright Brothers Master Pilot Award for 50 years of continuous incident-free, accident-free aviation. He took a four-year hiatus from orthopedic surgery and flew 5,000 hours as a bush pilot in Alaska. His initial operating experience was with Ryan Air 90 miles north of the Arctic Circle, out of Kotzebue, Alaska, on the Bering Sea during the winter of 1989. Ultimately, he earned his multiengine Airline Transport Pilot certificate.

Rock climbing has also been a passion of his for over 40 years. It all started in Salt Lake City in 1975. Randy and his partner, "Lobo," were self-taught and lucky to have lived through it. The following year, they took an ice-climbing class in the Wasatch Mountains and started a lifetime adventure. Soon cross-country skiing was added to the rock and ice climbing; it was the perfect storm for winter mountaineering.

Randy started downhill skiing in Utah in 1974. He won a gold NASTAR medal in 2008. His fastest recorded downhill speed was 66.3 MPH; one day's most considerable cumulative effort documented on his Epic Pass was 37 runs for 63,681 vertical feet. He skied more than 1,300,000 cumulative vertical feet over 43 days, of which only 33 were full days of skiing.

Lippincott is a 1968 graduate of Central City Highschool, a 1976 graduate of the University of Utah Physician Assistant Program, and a 1980 alumnus of the Montefiore Post Graduate Surgical Residency program in New York City. He earned a B.S. in Health Science from the

University of Utah in 1982 and a Master's Degree in 1999 from the University of Nebraska.

He has worked as a carpenter, walked the red iron as an ironworker, farmer, painter, real estate agent, airline pilot, in a car body shop, and worked 36 years as a Physician Assistant. His other interests are rock and ice climbing, downhill and cross-country skiing, sailing, kayaking, skydiving, scuba diving, fly fishing, hunting, mountain biking, rollerblading, and photography.

In the game of hockey, it's called a Hat Trick. In equine circles, they use the term trifecta. Religion refers to it as the Trinity. But in the case of literature, the term used is a trilogy. Randy has written three autobiographies. First on flying - *Fifty Years Fly By* (these works are a diary of persistence and dedication blended with real-life adventures and the uncertainty of a half-century of flight. The bonus - aviation stories frontier style directly from Alaska). On climbing - *Three Days Of The Condor*, and adventure skydiving - *Out Of The Blue.* Veni Vidi Vici.

Glossary

07K - Three letter designator indicating the Central City, Nebraska airport.

Alaskan Bush Pilot - A pilot for hire that services villages away from any road system or lands on gravel bars or the tundra for hunting and fishing.

AOPA - Aircraft Owners and Pilots Association.

ATC - Air Traffic Control. The government-operated aviation system.

ATP - Airline Transport Pilot. The license required to fly a commercial airliner.

B-24 - A four-engine WWII bomber aircraft.

Base leg - Part of the traffic pattern at 90 degrees to the final approach to the runway.

CFI - Certified Flight Instructor under the Federal Aviation Administration.

CFII - Certified Instrument Flight Instructor.

Checkride - Flight taken with an FAA-Designated examiner for a license, rating, or currency.

Crop Spraying - Application of pesticides via aircraft.

Dead-reckoning - Or pilotage, a method of navigation using a watch and compass (with an estimated or calculated ground speed).

Density Altitude - The pressure altitude corrected for nonstandard temperature. As temperature and altitude increase, air density decreases. It's the altitude at which the airplane "feels" it's flying, i.e., the true performance or lift of the wing.

Downwind Leg - Part of the traffic pattern, going with the wind, which is the opposite direction of the Final Approach, into the wind.

FAA - Federal Aviation Administration.

FBO - Fixed Base Operators. Where aircraft are serviced and fueled.

Ferry - A temporary permit to fly from A to B for repair with questionably airworthy aircraft.

Flight Service Station - Government facility where a pilot can obtain a weather briefing and file a flight plan.

Hood-time - A vision-restricting device to practice instrument flight.

IFR - Instrument Flight Rules, i.e., regulations for flying in the clouds.

MPA - Wright Brothers Master Pilot Award for fifty continuous years of incident-free, accident-free flight.

Municipal Airport - A city-owned and operated airfield.

NTSB - National Transportation and Safety Board. A government department that investigates accidents.

OAT - Outside air temperature.

PIC - Pilot in Command typically sits in the left seat of a fixed-wing aircraft.

Primacy Principle - Also known as the "Doctrine of Primacy." The primacy behavioral principle can be expressed as: "first in – first out." The first thing we are taught about something will be what we remember the longest – and recall the quickest. The first learned reaction to a set of circumstances will be what we do if those circumstances occur in an emergency, even without conscious thought. Dan Tyler

Private License - A pilot's permit to carry passengers but not charge for it.

Ratings - Add-ons to the private license include the instrument rating, commercial, multiengine, float, and type ratings.

Runway - Landing surface for aircraft that may be paved, gravel, dirt, water, snow, or a grass field.

Simulator - A stationary device that imitates flight. A pilot can practice repeated maneuvers without consequences or burning any fuel.

Solo - The first operation of an airplane without anyone else in the aircraft.

Trim Tab - Small adjustable surfaces connected to the trailing edge of a larger control surface to counteract aerodynamic forces without the pilot needing to apply pressure to the control yoke continuously.

VFR - Visual flight rules.

Wide-body Jets - Commercial Airliners with a wide fuselage to accommodate two passenger aisles. In the typical wide-body economy cabin, passengers are seated seven to ten abreast, allowing a total capacity of between 200 to 850 passengers.

Wright Brothers Master Pilot Award - FAA official decoration for 50 years of continuous safe aviation.

WW II - World War Two era was a global conflict from 1939 to 1945.

Printed in the United States
by Baker & Taylor Publisher Services